Barbados:
The Visitor's Guide

Sir Alexander Hoyos

A personal guide to the island's
historic and natural heritage

Recommended by
the Barbados Board of Tourism

MACMILLAN CARIBBEAN

First published 1982
Reprinted 1983

Published by
Macmillan Education
London and Basingstoke
Companies and representatives in Lagos, Zaria, Manzini,
Nairobi, Singapore, Hong Kong, Delhi, Dublin, Auckland,
Melbourne, Tokyo, New York, Washington, Dallas

Photographs in this guide are published by courtesy of the
Barbados Board of Tourism

ISBN 0 333 33389 6

Printed in Hong Kong

By the same author:
  Some Eminent Contemporaries
  Two Hundred Years
  Story of the Progressive Movement
  Our Common Heritage
  Princess Margaret and the Memories of Our Past
  The Road to Responsible Government
  Barbados, Our Island Home
  The Rise of West Indian Democracy
  Background to Independence
  Builders of Barbados
  Grantley Adams and the Social Revolution
  Barbados: A History from the Amerindians to
  Independence

Barbados Board Of Tourism Offices

BARBADOS
    Harbour Road
    Bridgetown
    Barbados W.I.
    Telephone: (809-42) 72623
    Telex: 2420 WB

CANADA
    20 Queen Street West
    Suite 1508
    Toronto, Ontario
    M5H 3R3
    Canada
    Telephone: (416) 979-2137
    Telex: 021-06-218-247

    666 Sherbrook Street West
    Suite 1105
    Montreal, Quebec H3A
    1E7 Canada
    Telephone: (514) 288-1200

    Macleod Place 1
    Suite 307
    5920 Macleod Trail South
    Calgary, Alberta
    Canada
    Telephone: (403) 255-7585

GERMANY
    Steinweg 5
    6000 Frankfurt/Main 1
    West Germany
    Telephone: 284451
    Telex: 041-414068

U.K.
    6 Upper Belgrave Street
    London S.W.I. X8AZ
    England
    Telephone: (01) 235-4607
    Telex: 051-915856

U.S.A.
    800 Second Avenue
    New York, N.Y. 10017
    Telephone: (212) 986-6516/8
    Telex: 023-666387

3440 Wilshire Boulevard
Suite 1215
Los Angeles 90010
California

Barbados Board of Tourism
Knowlebourne Square
199 South Knowles Avenue
Winterpark, Florida 32789
Telephone: (305) 645-4145
Telex: 025-808671

VENEZUELA

Quinta "Chapaleta"
9th Transversal
Altamira
Caracas
Venezuela
Telephone: 331518
Telex: 031-26442

*BARBADOS
HOTEL
ASSOCIATION*

Bush Hill
Garrison
St Michael
Barbados
Telephone: (809-42) 65041
Telex: WB 2314
Cable Address: HOBARS-BARBADOS

CONTENTS

FOREWORD

By the Minister of Tourism,
Hon. H.B. St. John, Q.C., M.P.

It gives me great pleasure to write a foreword for *Barbados: A Visitor's Guide* by Sir Alexander Hoyos.

Sir Alexander has been described by Professor Gordon Lewis as one of the most prolific writers in the region. For nearly forty years he has been writing on aspects of Barbadian and West Indian history and for his contributions in this field he was knighted in March 1980.

In this book, the author seeks to introduce his readers to the natural and historic heritage of Barbados. The book is a visitor's guide with a difference. It suggests a number of trips and provides detailed maps that will enable the visitor to find his way about, with this book as his only guide.

For the lovers of nature, there are abundant details about the trees and flowers of the island, and the wild, unspoilt beauty of the cliffs and beaches in the familiar and more remote places of the island. For the lovers of history, the story is told of the many historic sites in Barbados.

In addition to all this, a chapter is added on the night life of the island for those who want to be entertained by what is provided at the hotels, discos and night clubs.

Barbados: A Visitor's Guide should be of interest not only to visitors but to all those Barbadians who may not know as much as they would like about the beauty and charm of their island home.

I therefore recommend the book to all visitors and Barbadians alike.

AUTHOR'S FOREWORD

The idea of this little book was first put into my head some eight years ago by my friend, Bill Lennox of Macmillan Education Ltd. He said that I had so far produced a number of 'prestige' works which had brought me some fame but no fortune. He suggested that I should now write something with the widest possible appeal — a popular work that would introduce visitors to the island's historic and natural heritage.

That was in 1973. As it turned out, we soon became absorbed in the production of two books: *Grantley Adams and the Social Revolution* in 1974 and *Barbados: A History from the Amerindians to Independence* in 1978, and the suggestion of a visitor's guide book receded into the background.

The idea conceived by Bill Lennox was later revived by another friend of mine Arne Schmidt, a German travel agent, who has been based in Toronto, Canada, during the past thirty years. It was he who suggested the form that the book should take: a series of tours to the island's beauty spots and historic sites. He stressed that pictures were important but that maps were even more necessary for the guidance of the visitor.

The main object of this little book is to tell visitors as much as they want to know about Barbados. I also hope, however, that those of my fellow Barbadians, who do not know their island home as well as they should, will learn something of its hidden charms and the beauty of its out of the way places.

I am grateful to the officials of the Barbados Board of Tourism, particularly the Director, Patrick Hinds, and the Marketing Manager, Tony Arthur, for the guidance and assistance they gave me in the compilation of *Barbados: A Visitor's Guide*. I must also express my gratitude to the Minister of Tourism for the great personal interest he took in my effort to produce a book that would be a useful guide to the many visitors coming to Barbados.

To meet the deadline, my wife has been of invaluable assistance. She worked with unwearying industry to type not only the narrative but the index at the end of the book. For this and other reasons I have dedicated the book to her.

F.A. Hoyos

Especially for Gladys

Chapter One
A CONSTITUTIONAL MONARCHY

Where in the world is Barbados, the stranger from afar may well ask?

It is the most easterly of the group of islands that stretches in an arc from Florida to the northern part of South America. It is 2,592 kms (1,611 miles) from Miami, just about 3,220 kms (2,000 miles) from New York, and 3,908 kms (2,429 miles) from Toronto. To visitors coming from the other side of the Atlantic Ocean, it is 6,750 kms (4,195 miles) from London and 7,240 kms (4,500 miles) from Luxembourg.

Origin And Name

What kind of place is Barbados, the stranger may next ask?

It is an oceanic island, separate and distinct from the West Indian archipelago. Successively inhabited since the birth of Christ by three branches of the Amerindian family, it was settled by the English in 1627. From the latter it obtained its representative system of government which it has retained up to the present time. In all the wars of the Empire that have taken place in the Caribbean, Barbados is the only territory that has never changed hands.

It was the Portuguese, however, and not the English, who gave Barbados its name. They were struck by the appearance of the bearded fig trees on the island and from this, according to one version, it was given its name: Barbados meaning the Bearded Ones (Los Barbados). Some of these trees are still on the island.

The Barbados Constitution

1. The Head of State

Barbados is a constitutional monarchy with a parliamentary system of government. The Head of State, who is at present Queen Elizabeth II, is shared with other states of the Commonwealth, for example Jamaica.

Since the Queen is Head of so many states, most of her functions are performed by the Governor General who is her representative in Barbados. Legally, she has the power to appoint or remove the Governor General, but by a convention of the Barbados Constitution she takes such action on the advice of the Prime Minister.

The powers of the Head of State are not the same as those of an absolute ruler. The powers of the Governor General are exercised on the advice of the Prime Minister and the members of the Cabinet who are all appointed by the Prime Minister. The most significant personal influence of the Governor General may be his powers of choosing the Prime Minister and appointing a substantial minority of the Senate. This influence does not normally amount to anything because his choice of Prime Minister may well be narrowed to a single individual, following the result of a general election.

Government House

2. The Privy Council

An important institution of the Barbados Constitution is the Privy Council. This is appointed by the Governor General after consultation with, and not on the advice of, the Prime Minister.

The Privy Council performs three important functions. It hears appeals from civil servants and other persons subject to the jurisdiction of the Service Commissions. It considers petitions from those who have been convicted of offences against the law of Barbados for the remission of the whole or part of any punishment. It advises on the exercise of the prerogative of mercy where a person has been sentenced to death for an offence against the law of the land.

The Privy Council discharges its functions by giving advice to the Governor General and the latter is obliged by the Constitution to act in accordance with their advice.

3. Parliament

The Barbados Parliamentary system consists of an elected House of Assembly and a nominated Senate. It is therefore defined as a 'bicameral' system. The House of Assembly consists of members elected by twenty-seven constituencies and may be regarded as the sovereign power in the land.

The Senate is prevented from competing with the House in a number of ways. A measure passed by the House can become law without the consent of the Senate except where amendments to the Constitution are concerned. If the measure is a 'money bill' the Senate can delay its passage for one month only.

Also, the majority of the members of the Senate can be dismissed at any time by the Prime Minister who himself obtains and retains his office by the consent of the majority of the members of the House of Assembly.

Although the Governor General appears to have been given a power of veto by the Constitution, there is a clearly established convention that obliges him to assent to any legislation placed before him.

Thus the power of Parliament in Barbados is pre-eminent, for it enjoys the indisputable authority to change all laws and even to amend the Constitution if it can achieve the requisite majorities.

4. The Prime Minister And Cabinet

The real source of power in Barbados lies with the Prime Minister and his Cabinet. This is ensured by the Constitution which requires the Governor General to exercise his powers of Head of State on the advice of the Cabinet, or the Prime Minister acting

4

under the authority of the Cabinet.

Nevertheless, an attempt is made to limit the powers of the Executive in certain matters. The control of government by the Prime Minister and Cabinet is limited by the system of appointments to the civil service, the police force and the armed forces. They are made by the Service Commissions in order to limit the scope of political patronage.

Even so the influence of the Prime Minister is merely limited and never completely removed. This is clearly the case since the Prime Minister has a decisive influence on the appointment of the Governor General and of the Service Commissions. Yet it is a tribute to the Barbadian sense of fair play that appointment to various posts by the Service Commissions are usually made without regard to partisan political considerations.

5. The Courts

Just as the Queen is the Head of State in Barbados, so the Judicial Committee of the Privy Council in the United Kingdom is the apex of the system of courts in the Constitution of Barbados. As in other territories of the Commonwealth Caribbean, the Privy Council in London is the final Court of Appeal in Barbados.

At the base of the judicial system in Barbados are the Magistrates' Courts. At the next level is the Supreme Court which consists of the Chief Justice and three Puisne Judges. Substantial protection is provided in the Barbados Constitution to ensure the independence of the judges of the Supreme Court.

Thus Barbados proceeds with the day-to-day work of government in which a major part is played by the civil service. This is regarded as a non-political corps of career officers who, following the British tradition, serve governments of varying political complexions with equal impartiality.

The system we operate is of the essence of parliamentary democracy and is cherished by every patriotic Barbadian.

Further Reading
Barbados, A History from the Amerindians to Independence by F.A. Hoyos (1978).
Comparison of Some Features of the Constitution of Barbados with those of the Constitutions of Guyana, Jamaica, Trinidad & Tobago by Professor A.R. Carnegie.

Chapter Two

PORTS OF WELCOME

As visitors approach the island, they will be pleased by what they see from their plane. If night has fallen, they will be cheered by the lights that seem to illuminate even the remoter areas of the land.

The villages in the outlying parishes are quite clearly indicated. Places like Belleplaine in St. Andrew, Speightstown in St. Peter, Holetown in St. James and Six Cross Roads in St. Philip are all lit up. But it is the southern coast, from the Deep Water Harbour and Bridgetown to Oistins and beyond to the Grantley Adams International Airport, that stands out most clearly with its brilliant lights.

Indeed, the whole island presents an attractive picture, with pinpoints of light, almost resembling a star-lit sky in reverse, illuminated by brightly shining constellations in a clear tropical night.

If they come during the day, the visitors will notice how green the island appears and this forms a fascinating contrast to the gleaming white beaches that surround it on almost every side. They will see the different colours of the sea, with its varying shades of green and blue. Here and there the sea is so transparently clear that it is possible to view the sea-

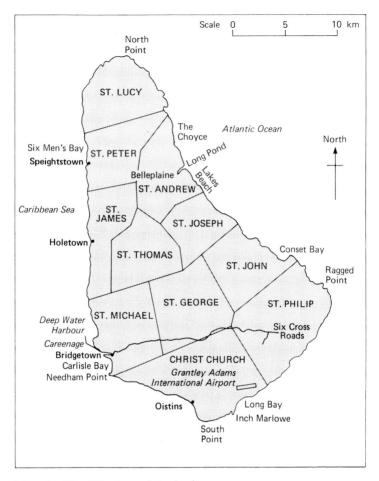

Map 1   The Districts of Barbados

bed at the bottom of the waters that wash the shores
of the island.

Visitors will note the white-crested waves constantly moving towards the coast and the coral reefs
clearly outlined under translucent waters. They will
also be struck by the tidiness of the island, as seen
from the air, and the trim, cultivated fields that make
it appear like a well-kept garden.

Modern Facilities

One of the two main points of entry to the island is The Grantley Adams International Airport where visitors will receive a friendly welcome. The airport is provided with an instrument landing system, distance measuring equipment, a beacon, radiating signals that will instruct pilots arriving from all quarters as to what course to fly to reach the airport, and a radar control complex, consisting of both primary and secondary radar.

All this has been done to meet the requirements of the International Civil Aviation Organisation. The Grantley Adams International Airport has thus been equipped up to the standard of the most modern airports in the world for all kinds of weather. Indeed, it is no exaggeration to say that Barbados now has the best equipped airport in the Caribbean.

The Grantley Adams International Airport

Rate of Growth

Perhaps the most remarkable thing about the airport is its rate of growth. There are at present about a hundred movements of planes arriving and departing every day from the airport and to this must be added sixty daily commercial movements. The number of persons using the airport is more than one million per year and it is estimated that by 1990 this may have increased to five million. This includes arrivals, departures and direct transits.

To meet these growing demands, a plan was rapidly implemented to satisfy the requirements of the airport. The length of the jet runway was increased from 2750 to 3350 metres. A new terminal building was constructed and all the necessary facilities provided with a minimum of delay. The execution of this development plan has entrenched the position Barbados already enjoys as the centre of air communication in the Caribbean.

Air Communications

American Airlines fly in from New York and Air Canada from Toronto and Montreal. British Airways take passengers to and from London, and Eastern Airlines to and from Miami. British West Indian Airways provide flights to and from all major destinations and LIAT does a vitally important service by connecting almost every territory of the Caribbean to Barbados. During the last few years 'scheduled chartered' services have been developed by Wardair from Canada and more recently by Laker Airways from Manchester, in the United Kingdom.

Then there are the airlines based on the island. Caribbean Airways, the national carrier of Barbados, fly to and from Luxembourg and then on to London. They also fly direct from Barbados to London. Caricargo (Caribbean Air Cargo Company Ltd.), jointly owned by Barbados and Trinidad and Tobago, now performs the services formerly provided by Carib West Airways Cargo Services and BWIA Freight Service. Aero-Services and Tropicair provide charters on request for business or pleasure, while Safari Tours operate one-day tours to the neighbouring islands, including the Grenadines.

In addition, there is Guyana Airways, which flies between Barbados and Guyana, while VIASA connects Barbados with Venezuela and opens the way to the rest of South America.

Barbados thus has numerous links with the outside world and these bring myriads of visitors from the neighbouring territories and from distant lands beyond the Caribbean. Whether they come for business or holiday, our purpose is to ease the transit of passengers by adopting the procedures employed at large international airports in other parts of the world. Our aim is not to harass the visitors with red tape but to give them a friendly welcome to Barbados.

Arriving By Ship

The other port of entry to Barbados is the Deep Water Harbour in Bridgetown (See the map of Bridgetown, No. 1 page 25). It attracts shipping from all over the world and is a rendezvous for innumerable cruise ships and pleasure yachts.

For three hundred years, ships coming to Barbados dropped anchor in the open roadstead known as Carlisle Bay. Visitors came ashore by launch, while cargo was transported by barge or 'lighter'. Lighters

The deep-water harbour at Bridgetown

were originally rowed by 'lighter men' but later towed by small motor-driven vessels.

The New Harbour

In 1961 the Bridgetown Harbour was completed and officially opened. It was constructed by joining Pelican Island, formerly a quarantine station, to the mainland from which it had been separated by about 550 metres of water. In the process more than eighty hectares of land was reclaimed from the sea. Thus did Pelican Island, once grandiloquently described as one of the Dependencies of Barbados, disappear from the face of the earth. Its site is now occupied by buildings housing the offices of the Port Manager and the Harbour Master and their staff.

The new harbour is situated on the north-eastern side of Carlisle Bay. It is about three-quarters of a mile north-west of the Molehead of the Careenage and thirteen miles from Grantley Adams International Airport. The new harbour provides 518 metres of quay space and about 822 metres of protective breakwater for ships. It offers four groups of berthing areas, can accommodate eight ocean-going ships and provide simultaneous bunkering for five vessels.

One of the important facilities offered at the new harbour is the Bulk Sugar Store built on reclaimed land and having a capacity of 81,280 tonnes (map of Bridgetown No. 2). Sugar is brought to the Bulk Store from the island's factories and then carried by conveyor belts through underground channels to the three loading towers from which it is discharged into

A member of the Harbour Police Force

the ships' hatches at a rate of 508 tonnes per hour. In addition, the harbour handles 447,040 tonnes of cargo and plans for expansion are being actively considered and prepared.

Cruise Ships

Of the thousand ships that use the harbour every year, about one-quarter are cruise ships bringing visitors to Barbados. Through Bridgetown Harbour, as through Grantley Adams International Airport, visitors stream into the island from many parts of the world. Many of them make an interesting variation in their holiday trip. Some come to the island by ship and leave from Grantley Adams International Airport by plane to complete their tour of other territories of the Caribbean and South America. Others arrive by plane and leave from the Bridgetown Harbour by ship to continue on their holiday cruise.

Further Reading
Bridgetown Harbour A Government Information Office publication (1961).
Official Guide Book to Barbados, 1980/81 A Dukane publication, Angela Zephirin (Editor).

Chapter Three

GOVERNMENT AND PEOPLE

Barbados is so eager to welcome visitors that they are provided with special facilities. If they are citizens of Britain, Canada or the United States of America, they need no passport to enter the island. But they must have some evidence, such as a birth or baptism certificate, to show their nationality and identity. If they have a return ticket to their country of origin, they are allowed to holiday in the island for a period not exceeding six months.

Visitors who are not British or North American have to produce passports, but no visas are required from those who are given a landing permit nor from in transit passengers who plan to stay in the island for only two weeks.

Facilities For Visitors

The Board of Tourism, the Immigration Authorities and various agencies do all they can to help visitors in the matter of health regulations. Smallpox vaccination certificates are no longer required from visitors. But certificates showing that they are free from cholera and yellow fever are required from visitors coming from the Middle East and Africa.

Another facility afforded visitors is in the business of driving licences. If they hold an international driving licence that is valid under the terms of the International Motor Traffic Licence, they are required to obtain a local driving permit rather than a local licence. The same convenience is afforded visitors who hold a domestic driving licence, if their country is a signatory to the above-mentioned Convention. But such a licence must be valid and must be registered with Police Headquarters in Barbados.

One last privilege may be mentioned here. Not the least of the attractions offered visitors is duty-free shopping. By a special law passed for the purpose, the island's customs regulations allow visitors to purchase many items free of any local duty. These items include liquor, crystal, bone china, watches, jewellery, perfumes, cameras and binoculars.

Other Facilities

Travellers may well have decided on the kind of accommodation they want before leaving their country of origin. To help them make this decision,

Public buildings in Bridgetown

they could make use of the facilities offered by the Board of Tourism which maintains offices not only in Barbados but in New York, Los Angeles, Orlando, Toronto, Montreal, Calgary, Caracas London and Frankfurt. In addition, it has information bureaus at Grantley Adams International Airport and Bridgetown Harbour.

From any of these offices it is possible to obtain information on accommodation, transport, currency, travellers' cheques, credit cards, banking facilities, entertainment and the many other things visitors may need to know about. The Board of Tourism also sends representatives to the main tourist markets of the world for promotion purposes and encourages writers who want to learn about Barbados to visit the island and gather material on the spot.

The Island's Atmosphere

As the visitors move away from Seawell or Bridgetown Harbour they will soon begin to savour something of the natural charm and beauty of the island. They will be enchanted by the scene that is presented on every side; the sunshine and the sea, the trade winds and the gentle rains that refresh the land; the one-time sea cliffs, rising in undulating terraces from the sea coast to the central uplands; the wild and rugged coastline in the north and the east that has so far escaped desecration at the hands of the developers; the winding country lanes and the quaint narrow streets in some of the urban areas; the Great Houses that still survive, recalling the era when Barbados was a slave society characterised by unprecedented prosperity with intervening periods of grim adversity; the numerous churches and chapels that cater to the social and spiritual life of the island

and indicate the deeply religious nature of its people.

Variety And Contrast

Visitors will be fascinated by the variety of churches on the island. There are Anglican, Methodist and Moravian, Roman Catholic, Baptist and Pentecostal, Church of the Nazarene, Christian Science and Church of God, Jehovah's Witnesses, Salvation Army, Pilgrim Holiness and Seventh Day Adventist Churches. In the midst of all this variety, there is one thing in common. Barbados is a predominantly Protestant country. Also, in addition to the Christians, there are such minority communities as Jews, Moslems and Hindus. They all dwell together in tolerance and harmony.

In contrast to the more prosperous looking houses of Bridgetown, Speightstown and other areas, visitors will see the chattel houses of the poor. Near the Great Houses, they will see the villages and tenantries where the labouring population live. And around the factories, some near and some far, are the plantations where the sugar workers toil in the hot tropical sun to harvest the canes when they are ready to be crushed by the sugar mills.

Yet it is appropriate to mention that, in spite of all this variety and contrast, there is a sense of community among the diverse sections of the community. They share a common language, a common accent and a common interest in the food and drink which are peculiar to Barbados and they are always ready to introduce visitors to their favourite dishes. Above all, there is the national wine of the country, the world famous Barbados rum which is relished by all Barbadians, irrespective of class or colour, who take great pride in introducing it to visitors.

Chattel house

Tradition Of Stability

If visitors linger in Barbados, instead of passing swiftly on to another place, they will learn much of the essential character of the island and of its people. They will be left with the feeling that things have been here for a long time. They will learn of the tradition of parliamentary government and the long-established institutions of the island. They will be impressed with the fact that, in spite of occasional disturbances in the past, Barbados has a long history of political and social stability and that this has proved favourable to economic activity and industrial progress.

Certainly, visitors will note the enterprise and self-reliance of the islanders and the reputation they have earned by their tolerance, their independent spirit and their law-abiding character. Perhaps, above all, visitors will appreciate the friendly welcome and recognise what is meant by the peculiarly Barbadian atmosphere.

The Tourism Industry

In the early years, the tourism industry was developed on a small scale, catering mainly to wealthy visitors seeking to escape the rigours of the winter season in their countries. Those were the years when Barbados depended on capital from overseas, mainly North America, to establish and develop the travel industry. For a time Barbados was open to the charge that tourism was making its people into a nation of waiters and maids.

Tourists participating in a goat race

Nevertheless, successive governments fostered and encouraged the enterprise of expatriates because they were aware of the contribution that the industry could make to foreign exchange earnings and to the generation of employment. A Tourist Board was appointed and hotels provided with such incentives as ten-year tax holidays which enabled them to write off capital costs over that period.

Foreign enterprise and government incentives have paid good dividends. During the past two decades, the Barbadians have assumed a greater initiative than they did before. The industry is now healthy and well developed and there is much local participation at all levels from the most modest posts up to managerial appointments.

Whereas the industry was once financed and operated almost exclusively by strangers within our gates, today the islanders are involved in the business of tourism and own a major portion of the various accommodation facilities that are offered the visitors. Some 15,000 Barbadians are employed in the various sections of the industry and an increasing number of them are playing a major role in the ownership and management of the hotels, apartment complexes and guest houses in the island.

Moreover, the natural friendliness of the people in the island as a whole has been an asset to those engaged in the development and expansion of the industry.

Settling In

As visitors settle in, they begin to experience the exhilarating feeling that they have escaped from the more sophisticated centres of the world to an island in the sun. They will learn, at first hand, of the effect of the sun as a source of life and energy. They will change almost immediately into suitable light clothing or don a swim suit and take a plunge into the crystal clear sea.

If they have not learnt of this before, they may well be surprised by the number of black people they will see on all sides. In a small island thirty-four by twenty-two kilometres, there are about a quarter of a million people of whom about ninety-five per cent are black or of mixed African and European origin. Everywhere visitors will find far more relaxed and smiling faces than they saw in their own country.

The Drama Of The Road

As visitors move around the island, they will see the drama of the road unfolding before them. They will notice, particularly in the out-lying districts of the island, that the road is used for many more purposes than it is in more developed countries. It is a social centre where people engage in almost endless conversations. It is a place for political and religious meetings. It is at times an open air club for dominoes, at others a cricket ground and at others again a football field or a tennis court.

If visitors want to get some insight into the life and

A game of open-air dominoes

habits of the people, there is scarcely a more diverting and instructive place than the road as it is used by the people of Barbados. If visitors understand and appreciate what they see, they will learn much. And, when they are ready to move on, a polite blow of the horn will quickly earn them the right of passage.

Further Reading
Barbados, Our Island Home by F.A. Hoyos (1960).

Chapter Four

THE HEART
OF THE CITY

When the visitors leave the new harbour, they will see
the industrial park that has been established on the site
that was once covered by the sea. Soon they are
walking or driving along the Princess Alice Highway
and then they come to Pelican Village (map of
Bridgetown No. 3) where they can purchase local
handicrafts of many different designs.

Pelican Village

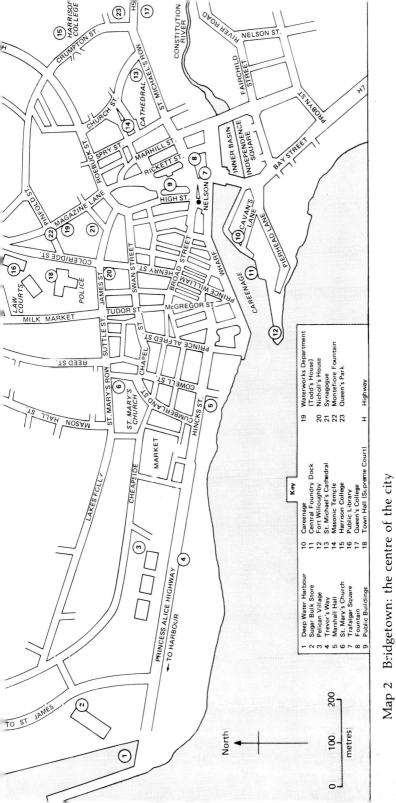

Map 2   Bridgetown: the centre of the city

Key

1	Deep Water Harbour
2	Sugar Bulk Store
3	Pelican Village
4	Trevor's Way
5	Marshall Hall
6	St. Mary's Church
7	Trafalgar Square
8	Fountain
9	Public Buildings
10	Careenage
11	Central Foundry Dock
12	Fort Willoughby
13	St. Michael's Cathedral
14	Masonic Temple
15	Harrison College
16	Public Library
17	Queen's College
18	Town Hall (Supreme Court)
19	Waterworks Department (Todd's House)
20	Nicholl's House
21	Synagogue
22	Montefiore Fountain
23	Queen's Park
H	Highway

A Mini-Park

On the seaward side of this Highway they will see an area which was once an eyesore. The beautification of this area was started by the Rotary Club of Barbados who, with the permission of the Government, undertook the task of its landscaping. It was planted with trees and named Trevor's Way after a young Barbadian who was killed in a road accident.

The Parks and Beaches Commission then took over from the Rotary Club and began the work of landscaping the area from the gate of the Deep Water Harbour to Trevor's Way (map of Bridgetown, No. 4). The cabbage palm and mahoe trees, planted by the Commission, are now flourishing and what was once an unsightly strip of land has been transformed into a pleasant little park.

Marshall Hall

As the visitors proceed along the highway, they will find a large building which is called Marshall's Hall. It is on the seaside and is situated at the corner of Hincks Street and Cowell Street (map of Bridgetown No. 5). It was a well known place of entertainment and attracted the notables of the island. Once it included among its guests Prince William Henry, who later became King William IV.

In more recent years, Marshall Hall had descended the social scale and was used, perhaps ingloriously, as a bond for merchants in Bridgetown. Today, it has recaptured some of its former dignity by being made the headquarters of the Barbados Development Bank.

St. Mary's Church

If the visitors retrace their steps along Hincks Street,

Broad Street, Bridgetown

they should turn into Cumberland Street at the end of which they will find St. Mary's Church.

St. Michael's Cathedral, which we shall soon see, was first built on the site now occupied by St. Mary's churchyard (map of Bridgetown No. 6). St. Mary's Church itself has some interesting historical associations. In its churchyard once stood the 'Justice Tree' near which, according to tradition, Sir William Tufton was shot on the orders of Governor Hawley and his Council.

In this churchyard, too, are the graves of famous men, including Samuel Jackman Prescod who was elected in 1843 as the first coloured member of the House of Assembly. Among those recently buried there is Ernest Deighton Mottley, the first Mayor of Bridgetown; a reminder of the days when the island's parishes and its capital city were administered by a system of local government.

As the visitors emerge from St. Mary's churchyard, they should turn left into Broad Street. They are now in the heart of the City of Bridgetown.

The Main Street

The City of Bridgetown is the island's capital. It started as a small settlement in 1627, then known as the Bridge, but is inhabited today by some 100,000 people. Those who settled in the Bridge were sent out from England by the Earl of Carlisle. His name is given to the Bay which is now almost deserted by ships but is filled with pleasure yachts riding at anchor or sailing up and down its sheltered waters.

The main street in the City of Bridgetown is gradually losing some of its quaint, old-world charm. Modern buildings have been constructed in recent years, with pretentious architectural designs that are scarcely suited to the atmosphere of the Bridgetown of old. Fortunately, some buildings, like those housing C.F. Harrison, DaCosta & Musson and the Barbados Mutual Life Assurance Society, have been able to retain their original character and thus serve to remind us of the kind of city Bridgetown used to be earlier in the twentieth century. But there can be no doubt that in the shops of this part of the city, more than anywhere else in the island, can be obtained a wide and attractive range of goods and all the facilities of modern banking are available for the visitor.

Nelson And Trafalgar

A pleasing contrast to the almost garish modernities of Broad Street is offered to travellers when they emerge from the City's main thoroughfare.

First, there are Nelson and Trafalgar Square (map of Bridgetown No. 7). A bronze statue of Horatio Lord Nelson, erected by the citizens of Barbados in 1813, stands at the head of Broad Street. It was

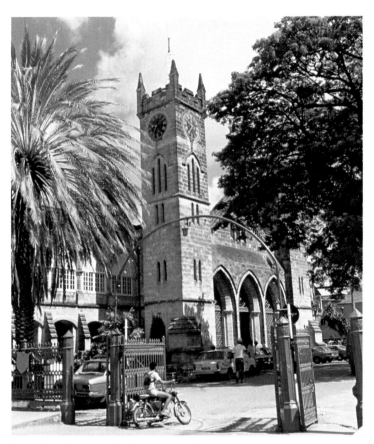

Trafalgar Square, Bridgetown

sculpted by the celebrated Sir Richard Westmacott
and is reputed to be a remarkable likeness of the great
English Admiral. In spite of the growing feeling, in
recent years, against the colonialism of the past, some
Barbadians are still proud to recall that Nelson's
statue in Bridgetown was erected twenty-seven years
before the Nelson column in London's Trafalgar
Square.

   Today, the House of Assembly north of Trafalgar
Square remains as a monument to its founder, Henry
Hawley, who has been described by one source as 'the

ablest scoundrel in early West Indian history.' With its Speaker's chair and mace and its Government and Opposition benches, with its parliamentary atmosphere and stained glass windows representing the English monarchs from James I to Victoria, it has for many generations been regarded as the House of Commons of Barbados.

It is interesting to note that Oliver Cromwell is depicted on the stained glass windows in spite of the staunch Royalist sympathies of the Barbadians during the English Civil War.

The Careenage

On the other side of Trafalgar Square is the curious little harbour known as the Careenage (map of Bridgetown No. 10). It is spanned by two bridges which separate its outer from its inner basin. One bridge is named after Charles Duncan O'Neal, the father of the modern democratic movement which has affected a far-reaching change in the political, social and economic life of the island.

The other bridge derives its name from Joseph

The Careenage and Duncan O'Neal Bridge

Chamberlain, the great Colonial Secretary, who saved the West Indies at a time when they were gravely threatened by the bounty-fed beet sugar produced by various countries in Europe. More particularly, he is remembered for the financial aid he secured for Barbados to help it recover from the ravages of the disastrous hurricane of 1898.

The Careenage is so called because it provided facilities whereby schooners could be 'careened ' and their bottoms cleaned and painted. It is situated in the eastern part of Carlisle Bay and can accommodate small vessels up to four metres draft at high water. It is equipped with one quay crane which is capable of lifting eight tonnes. Minor repairs can be done by The Barbados Foundry Limited on a small dry dock sixty-seven metres long, fourteen metres broad and three and a half metres deep, with a lifting capacity of 930 tonnes displacement (map of Bridgetown No. 11).

Not the least of the interesting things about the Careenage are the warehouses on either side of the inlet owned by DaCosta & Musson and preserved in their original character. Their preservation as places of historic and architectural interest has been rightly commended by the Barbados National Trust.

For three hundred years the Careenage was a berthing place for small ships from the various territories of the Caribbean. Few sights were more picturesque than the little ships coming and going, cargo being loaded and unloaded and passengers landing and boarding from the congested wharves of Bridgetown's miniature habour. Today, with the modern facilities offered by Grantley Adams International Airport and the new Bridgetown Harbour, it has lost its position as an important port of entry to the island.

St. Michael's Cathedral

St. Michael's Cathedral

As the visitor proceeds from Trafalgar Square along Constitution Road, he soon comes to St. Michael's Cathedral (map of Bridgetown No. 13). The church, which originally stood on its site, became a cathedral when William Hart Coleridge was appointed as the first Bishop of Barbados in 1825 and the real history of the Diocese began. For two hundred years before that the Anglican Church played no effective part in the life of the island. Little or no attention was paid to the welfare of the African slaves but when Coleridge became Bishop there was a complete change in the policy of the Church. He set about the task of preparing both planter and slave for the day of freedom and it was largely due to his efforts that, when Emancipation came in 1838, it came peacefully and without bloodshed.

In the graveyard of the Cathedral lie buried many famous men. Among these is Sir Grantley Adams, the first Premier of Barbados and the first and only Prime Minister of the former Federation of the West Indies.

On the other side of St. Michael's Row, behind St. Michael's Cathedral, are the Masonic Temple and Cathedral Square. Happily, the Masonic Temple has been preserved from the desecrating hands of improvers. Not only is it of architectural interest but it is noted as the original home of Harrison College which was founded in 1733 and was moved just over one hundred years ago to its present more spacious grounds.

The Cathedral, the Masonic Temple (map of Bridgetown No. 14) and Cathedral Square have been listed by the Barbados National Trust as places worthy of preservation because of their historic and architectural interest.

Further Reading
Buildings of Historical and Architectural Importance, Preliminary List (Revised July 1973) by the Barbados National Trust.
Some Nelson Statues by Neville Connell, *B.M.H.S. Journal Vol XVIII November 1950 and February 1951.*
Handbook of Barbados by E.G. Sinckler, published by order of the Legislature (1912).

Chapter Five

CURIOUSER
AND CURIOUSER

There are many other places in Bridgetown that will attract the attention of the thoughtful visitor. Hincks Street, on both sides from the car park to W.S. Monroe, is full of the character of the old City. Swan Street on both sides from Milk Market to High Street, has the distinct atmosphere of the smaller shopping areas of old Bridgetown. Off Crumpton Street are situated the Retreat, the War Memorial, and the Headmaster's house at Harrison College (map of Bridgetown No. 15) and the original building to which the College was transferred from Cathedral Square.

In Bay Street near Chamberlain Bridge stands Nelson Pharmacy, a building mentioned on the list of the Barbados National Trust as one worthy of preservation. This street, on both sides fom Dowding Estates & Trading Company to the Old Eye Hospital and one building beyond is described by the Trust as an area wholly to be conserved and preserved as typical street architecture of the island.

Among the buildings of national importance, as listed by the Trust, are Queen's House and the Public Buildings, both of which have already been mentioned, and the Public Library (map of Bridgetown

The scene in Swan Street

No. 16) in Coleridge Street. Those which have been designated as buildings worthy of preservation include the whole complex of Queen's College on Constitution Road (map of Bridgetown No. 17), Hanschell Larsen on Prince William Henry Street, the Supreme Court (map of Bridgetown No. 18), Police Headquarters and the Waterworks Department (map of Bridgetown No. 19) on Coleridge Street.

Highways And Byways

Things become curiouser and curiouser as the visitors continue on their tour of the highways and byways of old Bridgetown. They will see the Vernon Pools building at the corner of Marhill Street and Dottin's Alley, Barbados Hardware, Carrington and Sealy and Fitzwilliams Stone and Alcazar in Lucas

Street. Nicholls house (map of Bridgetown No. 20), with two equal storeys below a truncated third storey and its high gable roof, is an interesting building at the corner of Lucas and James Streets.

In other districts of the City are the Town Hall in Cumberland Street, the Grotto in River Road, the Ursuline Convent in Collymore Rock and St. Ambrose Church unobtrusively situated in a quiet backwater behind the old General Hospital.

Visitors will notice that not a few of the buildings mentioned above are in poor shape and it may well be that they will not survive unless the whole area is upgraded. It is heartening to know that the National Trust is actively investigating the whole situation and that the authorities as well as many private owners are showing an increasing readiness to seek its advice and guidance.

The Jews Of Old

The Dutchmen who introduced sugar to Barbados were Jews, many of whom decided to settle in the island. With their special knowledge and expertise they helped to make the sugar industry successful and may be regarded as mainly responsible for the Sugar Revolution which is known to the student of West Indian history as the first major social revolution in the annals of Barbados.

Indeed, there is evidence that the first Jews came to Barbados as early as 1628; one year after the settlement of the island. At first, they were submitted to certain disabilities, but these were greatly relieved when their civil rights were extended in 1680. When the 'free coloured people' were given the right to elect or be elected members of the House of Assembly in 1831, the same privilege was extended to the Jews.

Commerce And Religion

The Jews were noted for two things, success in commerce and the practice of their faith. So thriving were their shops in Swan Street that the latter came to be known as Jews Street. The first synagogue was grievously damaged by the hurricane of 1831 and a new place of worship was built on the same site in 1833 (map of Bridgetown No. 21). It must have been an impressive spectacle, surrounded by its five cemeteries and shaded by large overhanging trees.

Today, little remains to remind us of the beauty and harmony of the past. There are only three cemeteries and these have a sadly neglected appearance. The main building of the synagogue is still there with its solid outer walls intact. But changes and innovations have been introduced to accommodate various offices from time to time in the past.

The Reason Why

The truth is that, with the gradual disappearance of the Jews of old, the synagogue was bound to fall away from its original purpose. Gradually, over the years, it was tragically dismantled. Its four great brass chandeliers, hallowed by generations of worship and devotion, went to the private collection of a wealthy American. The painting that once decorated the ceiling is no more. But a happier fate was reserved for the marble fountain of the synagogue, its clock, its Chanukkah Lamp and one of its benches, all of which are now safely lodged in the Barbados Museum. Another reminder of the Jews of old is the drinking fountain in the green triangle in front of the Public Library given by one of their number, John Montefiore (map of Bridgetown No. 22).

It is perhaps unfortunate that the Jews who have come to the island in recent decades did not arrive here earlier. They came to escape persecution by the Nazis and found a haven of peace and quiet in the island. Had they arrived earlier in the century, the synagogue, one of the historic buildings in the City, might well have been saved from an ill-deserved fate. But it is not too much to hope that something will be done to restore the synagogue and its cemeteries to their ancient dignity.

From all we have mentioned above, it should be clear that visitors will find much in Bridgetown to arouse their interest and provoke their curiosity.

Queen's Park

After this, they may be glad to rest for a while. They will find the ideal place in Queen's Park (map of Bridgetown No. 23) which is only five minutes walk from the hustle and bustle of Bridgetown.

Queen's Park

Adjacent to the Park is the main building of the Ministry of Agriculture with its interesting south facade. With its Gate House facing Queen's College, the kitchen building and the bandstand, Queen's Park is notable both for its architecture and as the official residence of the General Commanding the Imperial Troops that were stationed in Barbados until 1906.

The General lived here in state with his Nelson Gate pointing, as it were, in the direction of Nelson's statue in Trafalgar Square, and the Governor's Gate through which the Governor of the island entered when he called on the head of the armed forces.

When the Park was handed over to the Parks And Beaches Commission in 1970 it was almost completely derelict. The trees, which had been destroyed by the hurricane of 1955, had not been removed and those which had been damaged had not been pruned to encourage their recovery. The buildings, which are of architectural interest, were in urgent need of repair.

A Pleasant Haven

The Commission set about its task with characteristic energy and enthusiasm. Queen's House was restored and converted, without altering the character of the building, into an exhibition hall on the ground floor and a small theatre on the first floor.

The bandstand was completely repaired. More trees, such as cabbage palm, spathodia and mahogany, were planted, special attention being paid to the north and east sides of the playing field. The open spaces and lawns were levelled and covered with tidy turf.

The steel shed was renovated and its surroundings

substantially improved. As a result it is now more suitable for a variety of functions in an environment that is much more pleasant than it was before. A special area was prepared for a children's playground which is equipped with swings, see-saws, a chute and a tree-house. This playground had been established around a giant baobab tree which is sixteen and a half metres in girth and was planted more than one thousand years ago.

In this pleasant haven, near the heart of Bridgetown, the visitor can get refreshments from a well-equipped restaurant, walk along the cool, shaded paths and rest on the benches under the overhanging branches of the numerous trees that have now matured under skilful hands.

Further Reading
The Montefiore Monument, *B.M.H.S. Journal, August 1940.*
Monumental Inscriptions in the burial grounds of the Synagogue at Bridgetown, Barbados. Transcribed with Introduction by E.M. Shilstone, London, the Jewish Historical Society of England, University College, 1958.

Chapter Six

THE MILITARY PRESENCE

If the visitors have completed their tour of Bridgetown, as suggested in the previous chapter of this book, they should now be ready to carry their explorations further afield.

From the Old Eye Hospital, which we mentioned earlier, we begin to see an increasing number of mementoes of the military establishment which once existed in Barbados. This old hospital building was once the residence of the Chief Pilot whose responsibility it was to guide in or lead out of Carlisle Bay all visiting warships and all vessels that brought supplies for the British soldiers stationed in the island. The Chief Pilot was employed not by the Government of Barbados but by the British Admiralty.

St Patrick's And St. Paul's

Opposite the Old Eye Hospital is St. Patrick's Cathedral which was rebuilt in 1897 in the early Gothic style after the earlier church on the same site had been completely destroyed by fire. For many years no Roman Catholic priest had been allowed to

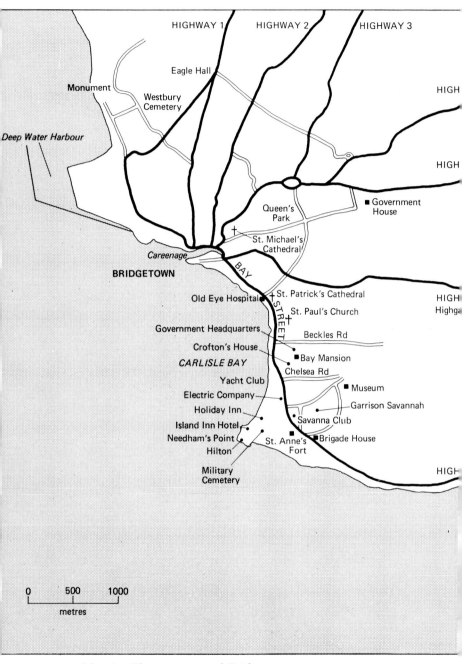

Map 3   The area around Bridgetown

reside in the island. This was the law of the land and was not changed until the Connaught Rangers, one of the regiments stationed in the island, demanded the services of a chaplain. When St. Patrick's was built, these Irish soldiers attended the services of divine worship conducted there and to this day their flags and regimental crests and plaques adorn the walls of the church.

Proceeding along Bay Street, we soon see St. Paul's Church which is well over a hundred years old. First erected in 1830, it was destroyed by the hurricane of 1831 and rebuilt the following year. At one time, it was used as a garrison church and its nave is still decorated with marble tablets that bear the names of many of the British soldiers that were formerly stationed in Barbados.

Bay Mansion

Near St. Paul's is the Bay Mansion, the town residence of John Beckles, a planter and legislator during the days of slavery. In spite of renovations in more recent times, it retains some of its old character, one of its special features being a gazebo built in the Gothic style and affording a partial view of Carlisle Bay.

Government Headquarters

After crossing Beckles Road, named after John Beckles, the owner of the Bay Mansion, we come to the Government Headquarters. This is a modern building constructed on mainly functional lines but it is not without a certain attractiveness. Certainly, its sweeping semi-circular driveway, bordered on all sides with poinsettias, begonias and hibiscus flowers, presents a refreshing picture of tropical colour and beauty; and this is heightened by the scene on the other side of Bay Street with the Esplanade providing a panoramic view of Carlisle Bay.

Legend And Fact

About a quarter of a mile along the way, the visitors will come to Crofton's House at the corner of Bay Street and Chelsea Road. Here, it was once claimed, George Washington, later to become the first American President, stayed when he visited Barbados. Unfortunately, this claim has not been established satisfactorily.

Washington came to Barbados on 3 November 1751, and it will interest the reader to know that this is the only country outside America that he ever visited. He was then nineteen years old but he was already one of the Adjutants General of Virginia with the rank of Major. He came here in the hope that his half-brother, Lawrence, would be cured by the island's salubrious climate of the grave malady that afflicted him.

According to Washington's Diary, he and his brother stayed in a house that belonged to Captain Crofton who was Commander of James Fort. The house which Washington rented at an 'extravagantly dear' price was 'very pleasantly situated pretty near the sea' and about a mile from Bridgetown. This general description tells us little of the actual site of the house occupied by George Washington and his brother. Such a description could have applied to many of the houses then in existence in that area.

The house at the corner of Bay Street and Chelsea Road derives its name from a tailor, Thomas Crofton, who was connected by his trade with the regiments at the garrison. He acquired the house a hundred years after the visit of the Washingtons in 1751. It is doubtful whether the corner house was ever owned by the Commander of James Fort. It is probable that the house rented by him to the Washingtons is no longer is existence. Here, however, we must stop for we have no desire to disturb the romantic who cherishes the legend that Crofton's House, and no other, was the place where the first U.S. President stayed during his visit to Barbados.

The Military Establishment

Obliquely opposite Crofton's House is the Yacht Club which is now a private club providing facilities for tennis, sea-bathing and yachting for its members. It was formerly the official residence of the officer commanding the Royal Engineers stationed in the West Indies.

As we go up the gentle incline, known as the Garrison Hill, we become more and more aware of the military presence which once dominated the social and economic life of the island. On the left is the Savannah Club, with its cupola tower and clock, formerly the Guard House of the considerable military establishment which was then situated in the area. On the right, where the Barbados Light And Power Company now stands, was a theatre where professional actors were engaged by the military to entertain the officers and men of the garrison and their friends. The money obtained from these theatrical offerings was given to charity in the island.

St. Anne's Fort

Further up, on the right, is the Drill Hall built in an

St. Anne's Fort

unimpressive style of Victorian architecture. Behind
this is St. Anne's Fort which was started in 1704 but
never completed according to the original plan. As a
matter of fact, the Drill Hall, built for the recreation
of the troops, was erected on the foundations of one
of the ramparts that was to complete the Fort and
bring it up to the road at the top of the Garrison Hill.
Today the main ramparts, which still survive,
indicate the ambitious design once planned for the
Fort.

Within the precincts of St. Anne's Fort is the turret

which was used to maintain communication with the Commander of the British troops in Queen's House and with the other signal stations in different parts of the island. Within the Fort, with its walls ranging from four to twenty feet in depth, one can still see the store rooms, the armoury and the powder magazines as they were when they were provided near the end of the eighteenth century to meet the needs of some 4000 soldiers.

Behind the Fort, looking towards the sea, is the cemetery where the soldiers who died here were buried. Not far away was Charles Fort then on a small island which is now joined to the mainland of Barbados. Charles Fort was allowed to fall into ruin and is now part of the grounds of the government-owned Hilton Hotel. It is to the credit of the government that it has endeavoured, with some success, to restore what it could of the delapidated Fort.

The Garrison Savannah

In front of the Drill Hall and across the road is the Garrison Savannah, described in its heyday as one of the finest parade grounds in the West Indies. This is now used for horse racing and other popular sports as well as for ceremonials, parades and other occasions. Around the Savannah are the arcaded buildings, built of red brick, which accommodated the soldiers and their dependants. Constructed by military engineers on mainly utilitarian lines, they nevertheless form an outstanding group of buildings with their pediments and arched colonnades that give them a touch of elegance.

Fort Charles

Main Purposes

As the size of the military establishment increased, Barbados became the acknowledged headquarters of the British forces in the Leeward and Windward Islands.

The primary purpose of the troops established in Barbados was to defend the islands from attack, especially from the French. Soldiers of St. Anne's Fort could communicate directly with the Lieutenant General through the signal station near Queen's House.

But there were other purposes which the garrison at St. Anne's served. With its signals system, connecting it with signal stations in other districts, messages could be relayed to all parts of the island.

Members of the island's Council could be

summoned to meetings. Alarms could be sounded if it appeared that the island was about to be attacked from the sea. News could be conveyed to merchants, planters and other citizens concerned about the arrival of ships bringing goods and mail.

Not the least important of its functions was to alert the white and the 'free coloured people' that there was unrest among the black slaves and that an insurrection could be expected.

British Troops Withdrawn

The British troops were withdrawn early in the present century and their place taken by the Barbados Volunteer Force. This was succeeded first by the Barbados Regiment and later by the Barbados Defence Force.

The latter has its headquarters in St. Anne's Fort and its present Commanding Officer is a Barbadian, Lieutenant Colonel Rudyard Lewis. It is integrated with the Coastguard and is capable of undertaking air and sea rescue operations, as required from a country with an international airport.

Further Reading
The Washingtons and their Doctors in Barbados by E.M. Shilstone, *B.M.H.S. Journal, February 1953.*
Imperial Forces in Barbados by C.P. Clarke, *B.M.H.S. Journal, November 1968.*
Tour of the Island of Barbados, W.I. by Edward Stoute (1969) (unpublished).
Historic Sites Re-visited. Crofton House. *B.M.H.S. Journal, August 1945.*

Chapter Seven

FROM THE GARRISON TO OISTINS

Evidently, the military establishment, which we explored in the last chapter, aimed at being, as far as possible, a self-sufficient community. Besides its barracks, store rooms, recreation centres, hospital and cemetery, there was also a military prison. This was located at the northern end of the buildings around the Garrison Savannah and is now the site of the Barbados Museum.

The Museum

At the Museum visitors will see Amerindian pottery, West Indian prints, antique furniture, glassware, fish, birds, books, newspapers and other records of the island's history.

In recent times, the Museum, under its Director, has aimed at developing an educational programme and raising the level of awareness, among locals and visitors, of the cultural and national heritage of Barbados. It had tried for instance, to provide better facilities for the development of the performing arts.

With this in view, it has improved and restored the

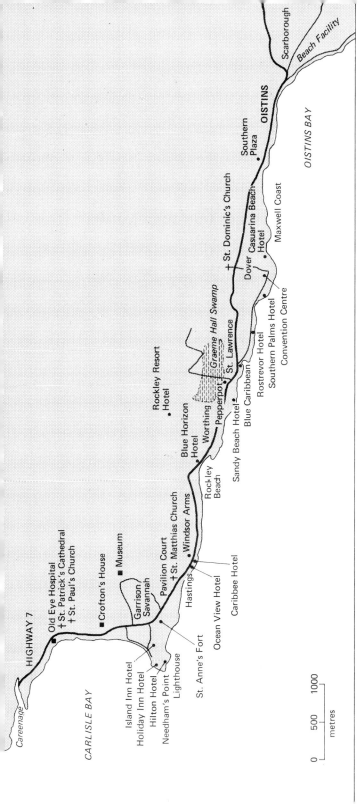

Map 4   The South West Coast

Barbados Museum

Museum's upper courtyard to accommodate a Green Room and storage area for equipment. This will provide great encouragement for such shows as *1627 And all that Sort of Thing* which is now staged in the Museum's lower courtyard every Thursday and Sunday evening.

A Caribbean Centre

The fact that such a show proved very popular has encouraged the Museum to provide improved facilities for performances that place appropriate emphasis on the history and cultural heritage of Barbados.

In addition, greater emphasis is now being placed on such things as the migration of early man through the Caribbean, the Amerindian way of life, the Arawak fishing village, the artifacts of the ancient Caribs, their survivors in St. Vincent and Dominica, the origin of the name Barbados and the settlement of the island by the English. More attention is also being given to such matters as the sugar industry, slavery, the Jews of old and the traditional crafts of Barbados.

The Museum is fast becoming a centre for conservation as well as a place of reference for advice on Museum matters in the West Indies.

Pavilion Court

After visiting the Museum, visitors should go around to the south of the Savannah and enter Highway 7. Here, if they turn left and proceed along the Hastings road they will soon come to Pavilion Court. This was built of red brick in the same style by the military engineers who constructed the barracks around the Garrison Savannah. It was once the hospital for the soldiers of St. Anne's Garrison but is now made up of flats occupied by private residents.

St. Matthias Church

Within a stone's throw is St. Matthias Gap which leads from the highway to St. Matthias Church. This Church was consecrated in 1850 and took the place of St. Paul's, mentioned in an earlier chapter, as the garrison chapel. The Chaplain of the Forces conducted a special service for the soldiers every Sunday morning, the British Government paying a sum of seventy-five pounds a year for this.

Ocean View

By now the visitors are in the heart of the tourist area where all types of accommodation and facilities are offered the holiday-maker. These include hotels, guest houses, apartments, shopping plazas and restaurants all along the highway from Hastings through Worthing and St. Lawrence to Maxwell.

The oldest hotel in the Hastings area used to be the Marine, but this is no longer a hotel. It is now called Marine House and houses a number of government departments. The reputation of being the oldest hotel in the area is now held by the Ocean View.

The latter was established at the beginning of the present century. With the help of Edward Stoute, its bar has recently been decorated with pictures of the area some eighty years ago. One of these pictures, for instance, shows the mule-drawn tram cars that used to run from Bridgetown to St. Lawrence. Passengers used to be charged one penny for a ride from the City to Hastings!

The Ocean View Hotel prides itself on the length of service given by members of its staff. It is known for the quality of its cuisine and it is significant that two of its cooks total a service of sixty-one years. Its handy-man, Dan, had been with the hotel for sixty years and is still a member of its staff.

Rockley Beach And Park

After passing through a heavily built-up area, the visitors will be glad to arrive at the Rockley Beach and Park. This is regarded as one of the island's great natural assets. If what they have seen on the highway seems to be a concrete jungle, they will recognise in the Rockley Beach and Park an oasis of natural beauty.

Purchased by the Government some twenty-five years ago, its attractions have been enhanced by the Parks and Beaches Commission. The area east of the drain that carried storm water from the highway to the sea was converted into a car park and the area west of the drain was transformed into a small woodland. More trees such as the immortel, the neam and the pink pouie have been added from time to time.

The Rockley Beach and Park are usually crowded at week-ends and, with the improvements that are being constantly introduced by the Commission, the area is certain to attract more and more people, both Barbadians and visitors.

The Commission provides a life-saving service at this as at all popular beaches. It advises that the sea along the western coast from South Point to North Point is usually safe for bathing. But it warns that when the winds blow from the south the sea on this coast can become quite dangerous. A more serious warning is given about the sea on the east coast which is nearly always dangerous except at a few places.

Graeme Hall Swamp

Just as we leave the Worthing area and enter St. Lawrence, a lane leads us from the highway to Graeme Hall Swamp. This is one of the few remaining swamps in Barbados.

Here we have an interesting tropical phenomenon. There are small trees or shrubs known as mangroves which flourish in spite of the fact that they are rooted in water. Since their roots cannot get air in the same way as land plants do from the soil, nature has provided different methods for this purpose.

An explanation of these methods has been given by Graham Gooding, a botanist by profession and a member of the Barbados National Trust. The red mangroves have long, stout stilt roots which are covered with pores that admit air to the interior and

Graeme Hall Swamp

downwards below water level. Another feature is that the seed starts germinating before it is shed and sends out a long, heavy root which can stick into the mud when it falls from the tree. Also, if this does not happen, it will float for miles until it reaches a mud bank where it can continue to grow.

Uncommon Plants

There are two kinds of mangrove at Graeme Hall: the white mangrove and red mangrove. There are only a few trees of the latter kind in the swamp and we have it on the authority of Gooding, that they are the only ones left in the whole of the island.

Between drainage ditches in other parts of Graeme Hall Swamp there are sedges, tall plants that grow a metre or more high. They are beautiful and rare in the island and it is believed that Graeme Hall is the only remaining habitat.

There are other uncommon plants in the swamp such as the button creeper with its pink stems and beautiful white flowers; and a tiny creeper that bears white flowers with yellow throats.

Bird Sanctuary

Graeme Hall Swamp is also remarkable for its birds. It is the only breeding place for the red seal coot which is unique to Barbados. The tall mangrove trees provide the chief roosting spot for the white egret. This is a beautiful snowy white bird which spends six months here to get away from the wintry north.

The swamp remains a sanctuary of the island's flora and bird life and there is reason to believe that nothing further will be done to destroy or reduce this area which is an important part of the island's physical environment.

St. Lawrence Gap

St. Lawrence Gap is noted for its chain of hotels, guest houses, apartments, restaurants and discos. Branching off from Highway 7 at the corner by the Blue Caribbean and passing the new hotel facing the window on the sea, it rejoins the highway at a point opposite the entrance to St. Dominic's Church on Maxwell Road.

St. Lawrence Gap, famous for its Dover Convention Centre, is a secondary road that provides facilities for visitors.

Fish nets drying

Oistins

The visitors, if they continue their tour along Highway 7, will see that Oistins is being rapidly transformed from a primitive fishing village to a regional centre for the south of the island. Almost two hectares of land have been reclaimed from the sea, from a point east of the beach opposite the Southern Plaza Shopping Centre to a point immediately west of the present fish market.

A little less than half of this reclaimed land is reserved for fishing boat maintenance. A slipway and winch are provided to help with the beaching of boats and a number of boat cradles to facilitate haulage. A newly constructed open-piled jetty will be used for several purposes: as a landing stage for fishing boats, as an easy method of transferring catches from the boats to the terminal, and as a means of passage for fuel, ice and waterlines to facilitate the bunkering of boats.

Within the terminal there will be facilities for making and selling ice to fishing boats to reduce fish spoilage. Here, too, fish will be gutted, weighed, filleted and stored. The fish, after chilling, will be transported by refrigerated vehicles to freezing facilities in Bridgetown.

While the fisheries development plan at Oistins is going ahead, recommendations are being implemented to prevent coastal erosion and to restore

The fish market at Oistins

eroded beaches between St. Lawrence and Oistins. This is rightly regarded as essential to ensure the success of the development plan of Oistins.

Scarborough Development

The plan to develop Scarborough, Christ Church, is part of the policy of upgrading Oistins as a regional centre for the south of Barbados. The building projects in this area will provide accommodation for several Government Ministries and Departments. There will be a new Magistrates Court and Police Station, a new Polyclinic to help implement the policy of upgrading the National Health Services and a renovated and extended Oistins Branch Library.

In addition, improved facilities have been provided for the new beach at what used to be, until recently, the old Coastguard Station. Improvements here include a new beach facility for the Parks and Beaches Commission. Increased car parking space has been provided as well as easier access to the new beach for pedestrians. All of this has already made it one of the most popular beaches in the island.

Further Reading
Tour of the Island of Barbados, W.I. by Edward Stoute (1969) (unpublished).
Barbados, Our Island Home by F.A. Hoyos (1979).
Report appointed to enquire into the present condition of Historic Sites in Barbados by B.H.M.S. (1910).

Chapter Eight

ON TO
SAM LORD'S

The tour suggested for today is quite different from any the visitors have attempted so far. It is likely to appeal more to the venturesome spirits than to those who are content merely to relax in the sun on the

Map 5   The South East Coast

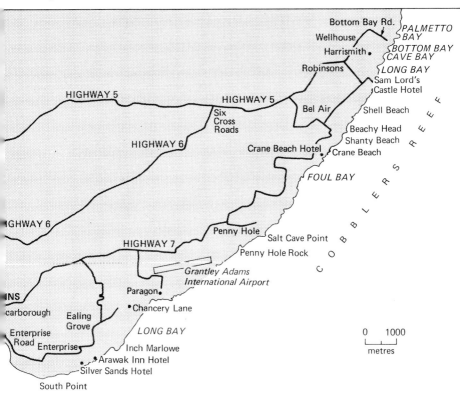

nearest beach. For they will have to travel along byways rather than highways to see, among other things, the sea rocks and sea cliffs on the coasts of Christ Church and St. Philip.

What lies before the visitors will appeal to those who are prepared to get away from their cars or motorcycles, walk along the cliffs, listen to the singing sea and look at its ever-changing colours. They will find that the sea rocks and the sea cliffs are vertical or near vertical, etched here and there into pockets, some of which contain fragments of vegetation.

Enterprise And South Point

Yesterday's tour took the visitors to Scarborough and the wide beach recently reclaimed from the sea. They should now proceed along Enterprise Road. Here, and along the way to South Point, they will see slight remnants of a type of coastal forest. An example of this is the thorn scrub which covers some of the low-level sea rocks in this area. Visitors will see the isolated specimens of shrubs which remain. Along Enterprise Road, for instance, they will find the sweet briar which, in season, produces fragrant, bright yellow flowers. Here and there they will come across wind-blown whitewood and manchineel trees. They should on no account eat the tempting fruits that hang from the manchineel trees since these are poisonous and can prove fatal.

Silver Sands

From South Point, Silver Sands is not far away. There we see a curious phenomenon that will be noticed elsewhere. As is typical of a windswept coast, the sand is blown into hillocks and forms dunes which are stabilised by vegetation.

A little more explanation may be needed here. The sand near the sea is very salty and few plants will grow in it. Among the few that do grow in this environment are the seaside yam, the seaside bean and the seaside spurge. These plants stop the movement of the windblown sand and others are enabled to take hold.

It is because of these plants that the sand dunes are built up. On the dunes the sand is less salty and a little soil is formed from the remains of decomposing plants. On this soil plants such as the sea grape and the dangerous manchineel become rooted and grow since they are not damaged by the blast of salty breezes.

If by this time you need a drink and a light snack there are two restaurants conveniently situated in the area: The Silver Sands Resort and the Arawak Inn.

Chancery Lane And Paragon

It should be quite easy for visitors to find their way by motor from Silver Sands via Ealing Grove to Chancery Lane. South-east of Chancery Lane is Long Bay, Christ Church, where they will find more sand dunes with vegetation growing on them.

After Chancery Lane they will come to Paragon which is south of the Grantley Adams International Airport. At Paragon they will see a cliff-bound coastline extending for about five kilometres. Moreover, they will enjoy the sight of the many attractive little rocky coves that extend for about one and a half kilometres from the northern corner of Long Bay.

Penny Hole and Foul Bay

When they return to Highway 7, the visitors can travel east until they reach Penny Hole (Gemswick). Proceeding along Penny Hole, they will come to Penny Hole Rock and Salt Cove Point. Here they will be presented with a magnificent view of cliffs running north-eastward.

The next attraction is Foul Bay, St. Philip, to which easy access can be obtained by following a number of byways. This is noted for its sand dunes, its vegetation and its undercliff wood. Like the Crane, to which we will soon come, it has one of the most popular beaches in the south-east of the island. The extent of Foul Bay is clearly indicated by the cliffs that run from one end of the Bay to another.

Shrubs, that are blasted and planed off by the wind, fare much better behind the shelter of the cliffs and sand dunes at Foul Bay and at the Crane and sea grape, whitewood and manchineel are quite well developed in these areas. But these could not be expected to flourish as well here as they do on the more sheltered west coast of the island where they show little of the damage from the wind blast they endure on the windward side.

The Crane

The next stop after Foul Bay must be the Crane Beach Hotel. By now the visitors may well feel inclined to pause and rest for a while. They might even be tempted to partake of the Pavilion Luncheon Menu offered at the Hotel.

As was mentioned in the previous chapter, the Crane is now the oldest hotel in the island. Started in the latter part of the 19th Century, it was once a

Crane Beach

shipping place and from this it derived its name. Its magnificent beach stretches all the way to Shanty Beach, Beachy Head and Shell Beach, though the athletic visitor may have to climb and descend steps to traverse the bays, beaches and cliffs along the way.

With its hotel and pavilion situated on a cliff overlooking the Atlantic the Crane has for generations been a fashionable resort for those seeking to enjoy the fresh sea breezes, the long walks on the beach and the invigorating sea baths.

The Local Poet

A local poet many years ago invoked the muse to praise 'this remote and hoarse-resounding place which billows dash and craggy cliffs embrace.' Yet his advice that visitors should 'bathe undismayed, nor dread the impending rock' should not be taken too seriously. For even strong and experienced swimmers have occasionally found it difficult to withstand the battering of the waves when they become angry and dangerous.

It would be reckless to assume, as the bard suggests, that virtue alone will 'shield us from each adverse shock.' It is safer, we suggest, to follow the advice given by the Parks and Beaches Commission to all and sundry, especially the visitor. Never bathe alone; never bathe after a meal or when hungry; never allow children to bathe except with their parents' permission and in their sight. This is the advice given to all bathers, not only at the Crane, but along the whole of the east coast from South Point via East Point to North Point.

When visitors leave the Crane, they should turn right and motor along Highway N, which is an extension of Highway 7 and, a few minutes later, turn right into Bel Air Road. This will lead them straight to Sam Lord's Castle.

Three Beautiful Bays

Before actually entering the Castle, we would suggest that visitors should explore a little more of the coast-line. From Bel Air Road they should turn left to Robinsons, then right to Wellhouse, travel past the road leading to Harrismith and drive down Bottom Bay Road. From here a track will take them to one of the most beautiful stretches of coast, consisting of Palmetto Bay, Bottom Bay and Cave Bay.

Captain Maurice Hutt, a member of the Barbados National Trust, has described this stretch as quite unlike anything else in Barbados. Palmetto Bay is a small bay, almost perfectly semi-circular in shape. Its cliff walls are vertical and rise some ten metres above the sand. Coconut trees grow on the sandy floor and their crowns overlook the cliffs.

Bottom Bay is a short distance away to the south-west and is similar in character to Palmetto Bay. Cave Bay has a larger expanse of sandy floor and is planted with many more coconut trees that approach the boundary of Harrismith House.

Sam Lord's Castle

The visitors should now be ready for the climax of this tour: a visit to Sam Lord's Castle. Lunch at the

Sam Lord's Castle

An aerial view of Sam Lord's Castle

Crane, may be followed by dinner at Cobblers Reef, the new restaurant set amidst the colour and beauty of a tropical garden at Sam Lord's Castle.

If they have not heard it already, the visitors will now be told the story of Samuel Hall Lord. According to legend, Sam Lord used to hang lanterns in the trees, on the horns of cattle on the beach and in the windows of the Castle to persuade the captains of passing ships that they had reached the City of Bridgetown.

Thus they would be lured on to Cobblers Reef and wrecked on the rocks. Sam Lord and his trained slaves would then set out to loot the wrecks. The spoils from the foundered vessels would be brought from the beach to the basement of the Castle through an underground passage.

Fiction Or Fact?

The truth appears to be that, before the lighthouse was built at Ragged Point in 1875, there were many and frequent wrecks on Cobblers Reef. A careful examination of the British Admiralty records seems to show that Sam Lord could not have been responsible for the wrecks that occurred during his time.

Sam Lord was out of the island from 1824 to 1827 and cannot be responsible for any wreckage that took place during that period. From 1834 to 1839 he was in England and cannot be accused of destroying any ship that was wrecked on Cobblers Reef during that time. And after the acquisition of the Pool and Long Bay properties he would scarcely have had to resort to wrecking to add to his material possessions.

In addition, no trace has ever been found of the underground passage mentioned above. It is not surprising, therefore, that those who have examined all the evidence consider that there is no justification in attributing the wrecks to Sam Lord.

What cannot be denied is that Samuel Hall Lord was a dishonest and ruthless man, determined to achieve his ambition for wealth and power. He cheated his family and treated his wife with abominable cruelty. But he cannot, on the evidence, be accused of being a wrecker. But who knows?!

Restored and Preserved

Long Bay Castle, as it was first called, was built not as a fortress but as the country house of a colonial gentleman of the early 19th century. It stands on a rocky cliff and looks out to a coral beach shaded by coconut palms and sea grape trees. And not far away are the reefs that form part of the legend of Sam Lord.

The interior of the Castle is beautifully decorated with woodwork and plaster work ceilings characteristic of the period. Equally attractive is the elegant staircase, with a handsome domed ceiling, leading to the upper storey. In the basement were the small dark rooms, once known as the dungeons, where Sam Lord is said to have imprisoned his wife. Those dungeons are how carpeted, air-conditioned offices.

It is to the credit of Marriotts, the present owners, that they have restored and preserved the original character of the Castle, with its interior decoration, its furniture, its crystal chandeliers and the massive and elaborately carved four-poster bed which the notorious Sam Lord used.

Further Reading
Report to the Council of the Barbados National Trust by M.B. Hutt.
Sam Lord and his Castle, by A.H. Wightwick Haywood, *B.M.H.S. Journal, November 1963.*
Sam Lord's Castle by Neville Connell, *B.M.H.S. Journal, November 1963.*
Four CBC-TV Programmes by E.G.B. Gooding, (1963) (unpublished scripts).
Regency Rascal by Lt. Col. W.P. Drury

Chapter Nine

ALONG THE WEST COAST

May we suggest that the next area of exploration should be the west coast of the island. On this occasion we shall have to travel along Highway 1.

The most convenient starting point would be the Deep Water Harbour. One of the interesting things we shall notice here is the shallow berth of the harbour to which the vessels that used to anchor in the careenage in Bridgetown have been moved.

The Wrong Date

Not far from the harbour a new coast road takes the visitors to Indian Ground where they will see the monument that was erected there in 1905. This monument was built to commemorate the tercentenary of the first visit of the English who claimed the island in the name of their King, James I.

Strangely enough, the monument has the wrong date inscribed on it. It says that Barbados was claimed by the English in 1605, whereas the correct date is 1625. Actually, this monument does not mark the site of the first landing of the English on the island. This I shall explain later in this chapter.

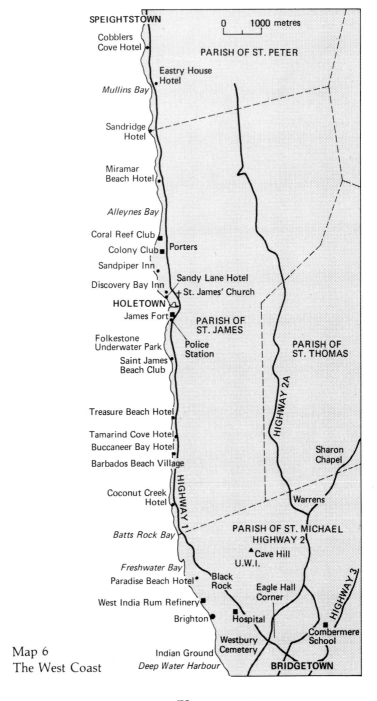

SPEIGHTSTOWN

Cobblers
Cove Hotel

PARISH OF ST. PETER

0   1000 metres

Eastry House
Hotel

Mullins Bay

Sandridge
Hotel

Miramar
Beach Hotel

Alleynes Bay

Coral Reef Club
Colony Club ■ Porters

Sandpiper Inn

Discovery Bay Inn

Sandy Lane Hotel
+ St. James' Church

HOLETOWN

James Fort

PARISH OF
ST. JAMES

Folkestone
Underwater Park

Police
Station

PARISH OF
ST. THOMAS

Saint James
Beach Club

Treasure Beach Hotel

Tamarind Cove Hotel

Buccaneer Bay Hotel

Barbados Beach Village

HIGHWAY 2A

Sharon
Chapel

Coconut Creek
Hotel

HIGHWAY 1

Warrens

Batts Rock Bay

PARISH OF ST. MICHAEL
HIGHWAY 2

▲ Cave Hill
U.W.I.

Freshwater Bay

Paradise Beach Hotel

Black
Rock

Eagle Hall
Corner

HIGHWAY 3

West India Rum Refinery

Brighton

Hospital

Combermere
School

Westbury
Cemetery

Indian Ground

Deep Water Harbour

BRIDGETOWN

Map 6
The West Coast

A Neglected Area

The area around Indian Ground, sometimes referred to as Indian River, is sadly neglected at the moment except by those who use it as a dumping ground for refuse of all kinds. A redeeming feature of the area is a creek with overhanging white mangroves. There are also two plants that are not found anywhere else in the island. One is a small shrub with shiny leaves and yellow flowers. Its petals are like little spades and at the base between these petals are pairs of honey glands. The other plant is the golden fern which grows in other parts of the Caribbean but is seen in no other place in Barbados except this area.

The coastal swamps along the west coast, with their special trees and shrubs, have long disappeared. They have all been filled in and the work of construction has gone rapidly ahead to meet the requirements of the expanding business of tourism. But visitors will find other trees on the beaches, including the poisonous manchineel.

Interesting Buildings

After leaving Indian Ground, we soon find ourselves in Deacon's Road. Here there are what used to be plantation houses. Rosemont was once the residence of the Medical Superintendent of the Psychiatric Hospital but, alas, Glenhurst, once the residence of the Assistant Medical Superintendent, on the other side of the road, has been razed to the ground.

From Deacon's Road, we move into Black Rock and we are now on Highway 1. Nearby, on the left, is the Psychiatric Hospital which is reputed to be one of the most up-to-date institutions of its kind in the West Indies. On Black Rock we also find two more plantation houses, Roseneath and Broughderg. And, if we deviate from the highway for a moment we shall see an interesting house, Brighton, one of the ancient houses of Barbados, from which the name of the road where it stands has derived its name.

Back on Highway 1, visitors will see a developed area extending from the parish of St. Michael through the parish of St. James and on to Speightstown in St. Peter.

A Closer Look

Let us, however, take a closer look at this area. Starting from Eagle Hall Corner, famous for its political meetings, and travelling towards Paradise Beach Hotel, we see one of the more depressed sections of this highway, densely populated and showing much evidence of poverty. But as we approach Paradise, we come upon an area that is more pleasant and more cheering. Incidentally, visitors may well think it a pity that Paradise did not retain its old name Freshwater Club from the beautiful Freshwater Bay of which it enjoys a clear and uninterrupted view.

Turning off the main road and ascending a curving hill, we come to the Cave Hill Campus of the University of the West Indies. This, with its hall of residence, its law faculty and its arts and science buildings, is surely one of the most handsome modern structures in the island. On the other side of University Row is the Centre for Multi-Racial Studies which is now closed but which, when it functioned, was associated with U.W.I. and Sussex University in the United Kingdom.

Going back to the main road and travelling northward, we soon come to the block of buildings, once called the Lazaretto, most of which is now used to house the archives, a repository of the most valuable records relating to the history of Barbados. Within this considerable compound is also the School of Education, an integral part of the University of the West Indies, providing an in-service training programme for the Diploma of Education.

St. James

After leaving the parish of St. Michael, we enter that of St. James. Here are seen the most obvious signs of opulence. There are well-appointed houses at the end of long drives, with trees and flowering shrubs offering a refreshing spectacle. And, between these houses and the sea are tree-shaded pleasances with massive walls to keep out the waves when occasionally they encroach too far beyond the high water line.

A west coast beach

At various points along this street are several hotels that cater to the needs of the more up-market visitors to the island. We shall pass them on our way first to Holetown and then to Speightstown. They include Coconut Creek, Westfort, Tamarind Cove, Treasure Beach, Sandy Lane, Discovery Bay, Sand Piper Inn, Colony Club, Coral Reef, Miramar and Cobblers Cove. Special mention must be made of two monuments to the memory of the late Ronald Tree; Sandy Lane, with which he was once associated, and Heron Bay, his residence. Tree did a great deal to preserve the heritage of the island as President of the Barbados National Trust.

The highway through St. James is also enhanced by the presence of the Bellairs Research Institute which is dedicated to the study of marine biology with special reference to Barbados. Established in the island in 1954, as an affiliate of McGill University, its aims are to improve the agriculture and fisheries of Barbados and to investigate and cultivate sources of marine food. Coral Reef must be proud to have such an institution as its distinguished neighbour.

Porters House

Opposite Colony Club and Heron Bay and near Holetown is Porters House. It is one of the few remaining plantation Great Houses of the earliest periods of the island's history but it has not been preserved entirely as it was originally built. Parts of the Great House belong to the 17th century but other parts were added during the 18th and 19th centuries.

The rooms of Porters are of different sizes and the roofs are of different styles. The furniture consists of invaluable antiques, with such items as a big dining table, a massive candelabra and characteristic four-posters. A long avenue of mahogany trees and a newly paved road give the Great House an impressive approach.

Once the property of Sir John Gay Alleyne, it now belongs to the Honourable Murtogh Guiness who comes to the house for a temporary stay from time to time.

The Settlement Area

Holetown is sure to be one of the most interesting places to the visitor. With its post office and police station, its shops and commercial banks, its cottages and apartments and supermarkets, it is an almost entirely self-contained community.

But as the place where the first Englishmen landed in 1625, it will probably arouse the greatest curiosity. It is here and not at Indian Ground that the English made their first landfall. Here they erected a sign on a fustic tree which lasted for more than 150 years but has now long disappeared from the scene. On the sign they inscribed the words 'James K. of E. and of this island.' Then they walked southward along the coast until they reached Indian Ground where they set up another sign, as we noted earlier in this chapter. The monument at Holetown, like the one at Indian Ground, has the wrong date of the arrival of the first English settlers.

St. James' Church

In Holetown there is also St. James' Church erected on the site where the first church was built by the early settlers. These settlers, eighty in number, were accompanied by ten Negro slaves who were taken from a Spanish ship which they had captured on the way to Barbados.

The church on this site must have been built of wood within a few decades of the first settlers' arrival. About two centuries later, the present church was built and consecrated in 1847. One of the remarkable survivals from the earlier church is the old bell, situated on a pillar in the southern porch of the present church. It is dated 1699 and has the inscription 'God bless King William.' It is interesting to note that this bell is older than the famous Liberty Bell of the United States which was cast in 1750 more than half a century later.

As the visitor wanders through the church among the relics of the past, he will see that among the mural tablets in the church is one to Sir John Gay Alleyne, already mentioned as the owner at one time of Porters House, and famous as the man who did more than anyone else before or after his time to establish the procedure of the House of Assembly.

Folkestone

Next to the Post Office is the Police Station behind which lie the ruins of James Fort. Only a part of the wall and one gun now remain where a sturdy fort once stood. Nearby is Church Point Cottage, on the site of Church Point Battery, and Folkstone House, once a fort for the defence of the area.

The land east of the house was landscaped. The Rotary Club North provided the apparatus for a well-equipped playground for children. In addition, changing facilities for those who wish to bathe in the sea were provided.

Folkestone, once falling into ruinous neglect, has thus been transformed into a very pleasant place for Barbadians and visitors alike.

Underwater Park

At Folkestone there is also an underwater park where the visitor can see the different types of marine life around our shores. This was started with the acquisition of the ship *Stavronikita* which was first stripped of all saleable material and sunk in the sea.

Holetown monument

Marine fauna and flora have begun to inhabit the sunken ship and already scuba divers are being attracted to the marine museum from all parts of the world.

All around there are facilities for jet-skiing and motor boating but such sports are not allowed in the areas that are marked off by buoys. This is to prevent activities that would disturb the haven of the underwater park.

Why Holetown?

Visitors are entitled to ask about the origin of the name Holetown.

The spot where the Englishmen first landed was called 'Hole' because it was like a little harbour or haven into which they could sail their ships. It also seemed to remind them of the 'Hole' in the River Thames with which they were familiar. Later the name of the settlement was changed to Jamestown, but before long it came to be known as Holetown again.

Today, it ranks as the island's third town, after Bridgetown and Speightstown.

Further Reading
A tour of the Island of Barbados by Edward Stoute (1969) (unpublished).
Barbados, Our Island Home by F.A. Hoyos (1979).
Some Early Buildings of Barbados by Thomas T. Waterman, *B.M.H.S. Journal, May to November 1946.*

Chapter Ten

FROM SPEIGHTSTOWN TO BELLEPLAINE

A few miles farther along Highway 1 we come to Speightstown in the parish of St. Peter. This was once regarded as the capital of the leeward parishes because it shipped all the sugar produced in this part of the island. At one time it did a great deal of business with the British port of Bristol and came to be known as Little Bristol. Indeed, even today, there is a link with the past in an old firm in Bristol, England, which is still in business and still carries the name of its founder, William Speight. He was the originator of Speightstown and appears to have been quite a remarkable man. He was a member of the House of Assembly which was established by Henry Hawley in 1639 and devoted a great deal of his time to the development of Speightstown. Credit for this public spirited enterprise is attributed to him even more clearly by the early name of the town which was Speight's Town.

Little Change

There has been little change in the appearance of Speightstown for more than a hundred years. You

Map 7 From Speightstown to Belleplaine

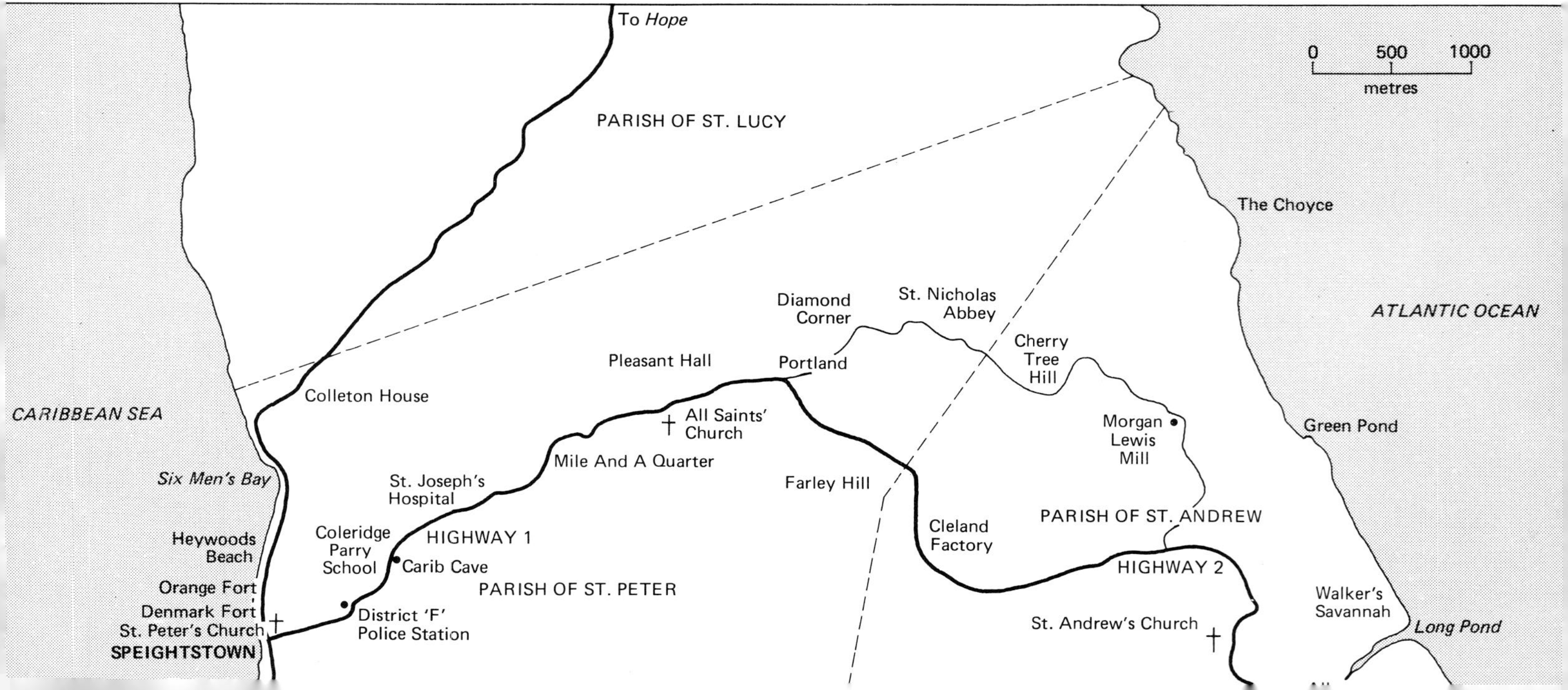

will see houses with overhanging galleries that represent the architecture of a bygone age. But they are not in good condition and may not survive long unless, as the National Trust has suggested, the whole area is upgraded and preserved.

One of the oldest houses in Speightstown is known as the Manse and probably derived its name from the fact that it was used for religious purposes after the main church in the town was destroyed by the hurricane of 1831.

Not the least interesting of the features that distinguish Speightstown are the forts that once protected it from attack and the remains of which can still be seen in the area. In the centre of the town you can see the remnants of Denmark Fort and Orange Fort which once mounted some twenty-three cannon between them. These were controlled by Dover Fort which was situated on high ground overlooking the town. Part of this fort is occupied by District F Police Station and the rest of it extends to the area near which the Coleridge-Parry School now stands.

Speightstown Transformed

Until recently Speightstown was described as a ghost town, but now it has begun to bustle with activity. New business enterprises have been established in recent years. Among these are Cave Shepherd, a branch of the big department store in Bridgetown; Reynolds Shoe Shop; Collins Pharmacy; a branch of the Barbados National Bank; a restaurant known as The Wheel; Straw Market, a branch of the business with its headquarters in the Norman Centre in Bridgetown; Exclusively Yours, a general shop with novelties, and Cracker Barrel, a branch of Super Centre.

A scene in Speightstown

The transformation that has taken place in Speightstown is due to the growth of the tourist industry, the extension of the Holetown development area and the construction of the Heywoods Complex.

It is interesting to note that Barbados is still linked with Bristol. Bristol Cream Sherry, imported from Spain, is blended and matured in Bristol by the firm of Harveys. Their agents and distributors in Barbados for the past thirty to thirty-five years have been J.A.K. Archer & Co. Ltd.

Recently a representative of the Mayor of Bristol

paid a visit to Barbados and presented a plaque to the Speaker of the Barbados House of Assembly, His Honour Burton Hinds as the representative of the parish of St. Peter. The ceremony took place in Speightstown and appropriate quantites of sherry were presented by the firm J.A.K. Archer to assist in the celebration of the occasion.

Outside Speightstown

Just outside Speightstown is Pleasant Hall Hill. There we can see Carib Cave where Caribs once worshipped. It is not true, as some scholars have suggested, that the Caribs only visited Barbados from time to time for fishing or to hunt for the wild hogs left by the Portuguese when they came here in 1536. They were permanent residents in the island for some three hundred years after they had conquered the Arawaks, but then disappeared from the scene.

Recent excavations have unearthed a vast quantity of Carib artifacts and this has proved to the specialists in the field that the Caribs were not merely temporary visitors but inhabitants of the island for quite a long period of time. This accounts not only for their place of worship in Pleasant Hall Hill but for the almost unlimited potsherds of Carib origin that have been found at various sites in the island.

Not far from Speightstown is St. Joseph's Hospital which was erected in 1966 by the Sorrowful Mothers of Wisconsin, U.S.A. It is a well appointed hospital with 140 beds and its surroundings make it one of the most peaceful and beautiful places in the area. With the chapel in its grounds at Ashton Hall, one can scarcely imagine a place better suited for the therapy of body, mind and soul.

After leaving the peace and harmony of St. Joseph's

Hospital, we pass the well populated district of Mile And A Quarter. About one and a half kilometres away is All Saints Church, the oldest church in Barbados. It was built in 1649 and in the churchyard is buried William Arnold, the first Englishman to set foot in the island. The altar tomb of Sir Graham Briggs, once the owner of Farley Hill, stands in the nave of the church and its stained glass windows also perpetuate his memory.

A mile or so along the way is Portland, a plantation house of many years standing. And not far from this is Farley Hill which was designated a National Park in 1966.

Farley Hill

Farley Hill was formerly the stately mansion of Sir Graham Briggs, once a member of the House of Assembly and President of the Legislative Council.

The remains of the mansions on Farley Hill

Some years ago it was destroyed by fire and it seemed destined to become a derelict of the not so distant past. Fortunately, it was bought by the Government led by the former Prime Minister, Errol Barrow. It was then restored and preserved for the benefit of Barbadians and visitors alike.

Only the walls of the once elegant mansion still remain standing. It is scarcely possible to conceive that it was once the gracious house in which Sir Graham lived in the grand manner. Here he entertained royal visitors and almost every distinguished person who came to the island. The house was surrounded by trees and shrubs of many varieties. The hall, which was decorated with Carib curiosities, led to a magnificent drawing room, connected to apartments over most of the ground floor. It was decorated with pictures, engravings and antiquarian relics, with books, maps and manuscripts of the rarest kinds.

According to the historian, J.A. Froude, a broad staircase led to long galleries which opened to bedrooms with cool balconies and universal blinds. Sir Graham treated his guests to West Indian banquets, infinite in variety and flavour, with wine that was as exquisite as the dishes, and fruit such as pineapples and shaddocks which, Froude thought, excelled all the other delicacies that were provided.

The Grounds Restored

All this now belongs to a vanished era. Farley Hill has not risen from its ashes to the pristine glory that was anticipated, but the Parks and Beaches Commission have done a splendid job restoring the grounds. The park for cars is sheltered by English evergreen trees and its border adorned with rare shrubs and flowers.

The view from Farley Hill

The garden to the west of the house is blooming with a variety of colour as it did in Sir Graham's time. The lawns are carpeted with zoysia and savannah grass. The restored walks, shaded by such trees as Barbados mahogany, tamarind, cabbage palm, norfolk island pine, travellers' palm and sago palm, lead to a ridge on the east of the grounds that stands about 275 metres above sea level.

From the gazebo and benches on this ridge the visitor is refreshed by the breezes that blow from across the Atlantic and by a magnificent view of the eastern side of the island. Below is a grove of undercliff woodland inhabited by monkeys. On the right is Cleland Factory with its arches and an old windmill. Further away is Walker's Savannah and the sand dunes that have made the Savannah famous. Then there is Walker's Beach, stretching from Green Pond to Long Pond. The spreading vista takes one all the way to Ragged Point Lighthouse which stands out clearly on one of the most easterly points in the island.

From Farley Hill one also gets a striking view of Chalky Mount which rises gaunt and rugged against the verdant hills and valleys that surround it. This is described more fully on page 113.

St. Nicholas Abbey

A mile or two from Farley Hill National Park is St. Nicholas Abbey. It is one of the only three remaining examples in the whole American continent of British colonial houses of the period. The second is Bacon's Castle in Virginia, U.S.A., and the third is Drax Hall in Barbados. All the other Jacobean Plantation Great Houses of the 18th century have been destroyed by hurricane or by the ravages of time or war.

The approximate date of the construction of St. Nicholas Abbey is 1650. Whether it is older than Drax Hall is not clearly established, though the old maxim about gables, 'early curly, later straighter' would seem to suggest that it was built at an earlier date than Drax Hall.

St. Nicholas Abbey, which is located partly in St. Peter and partly in St. Andrew, is approached through an ancient mahogany grove and behind it is a gully filled with immense trees and chattering monkeys. In front of the house is a stone-bordered garden which is typical of the English country mansion of the Jacobean period. Happily, the facade of the Abbey has been preserved intact over the years, with its three curvilinear gables. In addition, there is a single longitudinal gable and three long gables extending over the rear of the building.

Special Attractions

A curious feature of the Abbey is the fire places in the upstairs rooms and the chimneys, one in each corner of the building. These were obviously designed to cope with the conditions of a colder climate such as the architect had left in England in the 1640s. It may well be that the climate was not expected to be of the usual tropical warmth since the house was situated more than 245 metres above sea level.

Two additions made to the house in later years by Sir John Gay Alleyne were the porch at the front and the Chinese Chippendale staircase. Sir John, the

St. Nicholas Abbey

aristocrat and radical, once owned the Abbey and, although he died in 1801, is still remembered as the Speaker of the House of Assembly for thirty years.

One of the special attractions of the house is its furniture which is typical of what was used in the 18th and 19th centuries. Some of the furniture has been in the house since 1810, but much of it has been collected in Barbados or transported from his home in England by the present owner, Lieutenant Colonel Stephen Cave.

Five generations of Caves have owned the Abbey for more than 150 years, but the Colonel is the first of his family to live in the Abbey. At his request, the house was declared open to the public in January 1980 by Prime Minister Tom Adams. Colonel Cave now serves as the gracious host to the many visitors, both local and overseas, who come to see the house, garden and plantation yard of the Abbey.

Tale Of Tragedy

The house, which is almost as old as the recorded history of Barbados, is not without its tale of tragedy.

It appears that the man who built St. Nicholas Abbey was Colonel Benjamin Berringer and it is possible that he was the first owner of the property. His neighbour and friend was John (later Sir John) Yeamans and the two men were partners in the real estate business. When Yeamans began to pay attention to Mrs. Berringer, he and her husband became bitter enemies. It due course, Yeamans, according to one source, resolved to 'compass the death' of his former friend. They fought a duel and Berringer was killed.

Soon after, Sir John married Mrs. Berringer and took over the ownership of the Abbey. He used his influence, it seems, to prevent the holding of an inquest into the circumstances of Berringer's death. But the disposition of the Abbey was a different matter. A court of inquiry was held and justice was done when the property was assigned to Berringer's children. The property was later named after a grand-daughter of Benjamin Berringer who married George Nicholas.

Sir John and Berringer's widow, now Lady Yeamans, decided to join the first settlers who left Barbados in 1669. They were among the pioneers who established South Carolina, U.S.A., and later Sir John became Governor of that settlement in 1672. Two years later, he died and his widow, as light-hearted as ever, married again; for the third time.

Drax Hall And Other Houses

Drax Hall, which is in the parish of St. George, and which was mentioned earlier in this chapter, is occupied by a private resident and is not usually open to visitors. Once a year, however, the Barbados National Trust is allowed to include it in its Open House Programme.

Owing to the enterpise of the Trust, a number of other interesting houses are opened to visitors and locals alike. For the convenience of those who want to avail themselves of these opportunities, the Barbados Transport Co-operative Society provides a special service from such hotels as the Southern Palms, Sand Acres, Accra Beach, Caribee and Hilton on the south coast and Sandy Lane, Coral Reef and Barbados Beach Village on the west coast.

On To Belleplaine

But let us return to our tour. After leaving St. Nicholas Abbey, visitors should turn to the left and proceed along a road lined with mahogany and casuarina trees. It is a quiet, peaceful road and the branches that interlock overhead give one the impression of being in a cathedral-like grove.

Cherry Tree Hill

Soon the visitors arrive at Cherry Tree Hill. If they feel energetic enough, they should climb the hill; but the ascent is steep and covered with loose stones and, if they are not careful, they will come down faster than they went up. From the summit of Cherry Tree Hill visitors will be presented with a view that is as impressive as the one they have seen from the ridge of Farley Hill.

Morgan Lewis Mill

A few minutes later, the visitors arrive at Morgan Lewis Mill. Of the more than 500 mills that once worked in Barbados, not one is in operation today. There are many ruins still to be seen in the island, but Morgan Lewis Mill is the only one that is preserved with its sails intact. The Barbados National Trust has managed to acquire ownership of the Mill in order to ensure its preservation. To make it more interesting to visitors the Trust has established a permanent exhibition at the Mill of machinery, including such things as ladles and yokes, which was used to produce sugar in the days when the industry was operated by windpower.

Morgan Lewis Mill

St. Andrew's Church

Not far away is St. Andrew's Church which survived
the disastrous hurricanes of 1780 and 1831. Later it
was declared unsafe owing to its age and had to be
taken down. Rebuilding started in 1846 and, when it
was finished nine years later, it provided accommodation, as it still does, for 1,000 worshippers.
Unfortunately, when the parsonage was destroyed
in 1831, valuable material such as slave registers
and other documents were lost in the hurricane.

A Thriving Centre

Soon we are in Belleplaine. Here we pass the Alleyne

School which owes its existence to the vision and generosity of Sir John Gay Alleyne. Today, Belleplaine is a thriving centre which caters to the needs not only of the people of the area but of holiday-makers from Cattle Wash and Bathsheba. It was once the end of the line for the Barbados Government Railway which, until the mid 1930s, connected Bridgetown with outlying districts of the island. It is appropriate, I think, to make this the end of the line for our present tour.

Further Reading
The English in the West Indies by J.A. Froude (1888).
Barbados Diocesan History by J.E. Reece and C.G. Clark-Hunt (1925).
Some Early Buildings of Barbados by Thomas T. Waterman, *B.M.H.S. Journal, May 1964.*

Chapter Eleven

THE UNSPOILT BEAUTY OF THE NORTH AND EAST

We propose that in this tour visitors should take in the wild, unspoilt and sometimes rugged beauty of the north and east of the island. As in the previous tour, they should start from Speightstown. Since there are no restaurants in this area they might well be advised to provide themselves with a picnic lunch from Mullins Beach Bar, Greensleeves or Chateau Creole, or one of the shops in Speightstown itself.

Heywoods To Colleton

Before they leave the environs of Speightstown, they will see the Heywoods development plan. A 308-room complex is being constructed here and the project is owned by a government corporation. It is significant that the hotels and 'apartels' to accommodate tourists will be leased to Barbadians, who will operate them.

It is equally significant that no building will be erected on the sea side of the road. A path for pedestrians and a conveniently located car park will enable the general public to continue to enjoy the benefits of the extremely popular Heywoods Beach.

Map 8   The North and East Coasts

A view of the eastern coastline

After leaving Speightstown, the first port of call should be Six Men's Bay. This was once a lively whaling centre. But it is now almost completely deserted except for a few fishing boats. If visitors then travel along Colleton Hill they will come to Colleton House, conspicuous not only for its long drive and ancient mansion, but for its 18th century stables.

Terraces And Cliffs

Soon the visitors will reach the parish church of St. Lucy, which was built after the hurricane of 1831. If they turn to the right, they will see Alleynedale which is another Great House of the past. It was built in the middle of the 18th century with slave labour, like all of its contemporaries. It is noted for its great hedges of sweet lime and its palladian windows give it a remarkable appearance.

We would invite the visitors' attention, also, to some of the most beautiful seascape in the island. They will see, among other things, the high cliffs that run through St. James and St. Peter reaching their highest point in St. Lucy. The lower cliff, which runs from Cave Hill behind Lascelles and Speightstown, is said to be 130,000 years old. The middle terrace through St. James and St. Peter is about 300,000 years old, while the sea cliffs of St. Lucy are more than 500,000 years old.

Maycock's Bay

The first place to be visited on the north-west of St. Lucy is Maycock's Bay. This is a small but beautiful bay, stretching for about a mile along the shore. Its width is only about sixty to ninety metres. There is a balanced rock standing on a small promontory under the cliff which extends to the southern limits of what was once the U.S. Naval Facility at Harrison Point. This is now occupied by the Barbados Defence Force and its facilities are used to train young people not only in disciplined habits but also in skills that will equip them for gainful employment.

There are two steep tracks that lead to the beach, one of them descending to Maycock's Fort, now unfortunately in ruins. It is suggested by Hutt that these tracks should not be made practicable for vehicles which, through wear and tear, could damage the character of this small but beautiful area. There is ample flat sour grass pasture on the escarpment near one of the access tracks and it has been recommended that cars be required to park in an area to be laid out there for that purpose.

It is a pity that all the guns of the Fort have been

removed, though this does not detract from the picturesque nature of the Bay. Legend had it that there is a treasure buried in the sand floor. And nearby to the south is a bay known by the sinister name of Hangman's Bay.

Little Bay To Jones Bay

There is another area of magnificent cliff scenery extending from Little Bay to Jones Bay in St. Lucy. Especially attractive are Chandler Bay and Laycock Bay which enhance the beauty of this area. The whole of this coastal area is easily explored. During the dry season motorists have no difficulty in traversing the tracks that lead to the area; but during the rainy season the visitor has to drive with greater care and caution.

Gay's Cove To The Choyce

This has been described by Hutt as an area of exceptionally fine natural scenery, wild and rugged. According to the same authority, its coastal frontage extends for about five kilometres from Cuckold's Point to Green Pond where it links up with the Walker's Savannah area.

Visitors may well agree that Cove Bay is the most beautiful and the most deeply indented bay in Barbados. They will be impressed with the sight of Pico Teneriffe rising eighty metres above sea level. They will see it as a sharp-pointed pyramid crowned with a larger vertical rock. Cove Bay and Pico Teneriffe together provide a picture of almost indescribable natural beauty. The same thing can be said of the view from Paul's Point to the south across Cove Bay and beyond to Choyce.

A game of beach cricket

From Conset Bay To The Chair

Here we should leave the north of the island and proceed along the eastern coastline. In an earlier chapter we looked at the area from Chalky Mount to the East Coast Road. Here we may add Cambridge Hill, which is commonly known as Fat Pork Hill and which is situated north of the two popular holiday resorts, Cattle Wash and Bathsheba. The latter we have already seen in a previous tour.

If the visitors have not already had enough for one tour, they could travel further south and look at the coastal strip running from Conset Bay in St. John, past Conset Point and on to Cummins Hole and Skeete's Bay, a fishing bay with a small fish market close by.

Continuing along the same strip they will see Culpepper Island, the only remaining 'dependency' of Barbados. Here the visitors will be rewarded with the spectacle of some interesting coastal features with fine cliff secenery that is fortunately still unspoilt.

On the escarpment line leading out to Ragged Point with its lighthouse still standing, the visitors will see some rugged terrain of considerable interest. After passing Ragged Point, they soon reach Deebles Point and the impressive vertical cliffs that continue all the way to the Chair. At this point in the parish of St. Philip, we bring this tour to an end.

Prime Minister's Assurance

Recently, the Prime Minister of Barbados declared the entire coastline from Archer's Bay in St. Lucy to Ragged Point in St. Philip to be a National Park. This will ensure that the people of Barbados as well as visitors to the island will be able to enjoy our natural beauties and superb vistas, unspoilt by any plans for development in the future.

This assurance is a source of great encouragement to the Barbados National Trust in their efforts to preserve the natural heritage of this island.

Further Reading

Report to the Council of the National Trust by Maurice Hutt (1975).

The Barbados Handbook by E.G. Sinckler (1912).

Address by the Rt. Hon. J.M.G. Adams, Prime Minister and Minister of Finance and Planning on the occasion of the opening of the Rockley Resort Hotel Golf Course (3 December 1980).

Chapter Twelve

TO WARREN'S AND BEYOND

It is suggested that for this tour the visitors should set out from Bridgetown. Starting from Broad Street they should turn right into Milk Market and Tudor Street, passing into Baxter's Road. The latter is the street in the city that never sleeps. Here visitors and locals are attracted in their hundreds to taste the fish that is sold in the road, or rather in one of its byways. The fish is fried in the street and the customers line up in patient queues to obtain their succulent portions.

Travelling northward, the visitor soon reaches Eagle Hall which really marks the beginning of Highway Two. Before they get very far, they will pass several places of interest. On the left at Spooner's Hill, they will see Tyrol Cot, the home of the late Sir Grantley Adams, of whom mention has already been made. On the right, a little farther along the way, they will see Codrington House, 300 years ago the residence of the grandfather of Christopher Codrington of whom more will be heard in a later chapter. On the road to the right is the National Stadium and near it is Combermere School, one of the island's leading secondary schools.

Back on Highway 2, the visitors first stop could be

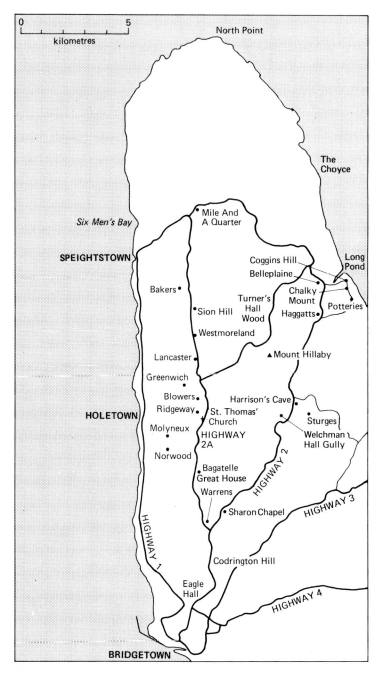

Map 9   To Warren's and Beyond: a tour using Highways 2
and 2A

105

Warren's, an old plantation house that was built in 1686. It is carefully preserved by its present owners, C.O. Williams Construction Company. The house is thus kept in excellent condition and is noted for its rather severe type of architecture and its high walls.

To the east of Warren's House is one of the few baobab trees still surviving in the island. It is not as large as the one we have seen in Queen's Park, Bridgetown, but its girth is much greater than its branches. Captain Maurice Hutt, a Council member of the Barbados National Trust, has recommended a list of areas of natural beauty and ecological importance and it is interesting to learn that he includes, among his suggestions, the preservation of this baobab tree.

Bagatelle Great House

For this part of the tour, we suggest that the visitors pass Warren's House on their right and travel along Highway 2A. They are now on the road that leads to St. Thomas' Church. Half-way along the road, they will come to Bagatelle Great House which is noted for the dinners it serves and still more for its association with the history of Barbados.

It goes as far back in time as St. Nicholas' Abbey and Drax Hall. It was originally owned by the Earl of Carlisle who was once the proprietor of the whole island. In 1651 the property was handed over to Lord Willoughby of Parham and its name was changed to Parham Park House. After a period of misfortune, Charles II rewarded him for his support of the Royalist cause by restoring him to the governorship of Barbados and all the Caribbean Islands. Unfortunately, he was drowned off Guadeloupe when his ship was caught in a hurricane in 1665.

Perhaps it may be added, without any indelicacy, that in 1877 the property changed hands as a result of a gambling debt and its name was changed to Bagatelle. The Great House is now owned by Nicholas Hudson, who, with pardonable pride, flaunts a picture of Lord Willoughby on the souvenir menus he presents to his guests.

St. Thomas' Church

Several kilometres along the road is the parish church of St. Thomas. No church in the island has suffered more from hurricanes than St. Thomas. It was destroyed by the hurricane of 1675 and rebuilt five years later. It was damaged by the storm of 1731 and completely destroyed by the great hurricane of 1780. It was destroyed by a similar catastrophe in 1831.

It is surprising that, in spite of all these misfortunes, much valuable information has been preserved in the register books of the parish church.

All along this route, the visitors pass one plantation after another. They will drive past Norwood and Molyneux, Ridgeway, Blowers and Greenwich, Lancaster, Westmoreland and Sion Hill, until they come to Bakers, in the parish of St. Peter, noted for its orchard, its mahogany woodland and its monkeys. They will be impressed by the charm of old buildings, the fields of sugar cane, the lush vegetation, the quaint country roads and the terraces, once sea cliffs, that rise from the sea on their left to the uplands on their right. If they continue to drive northwards, they will reach Mile And A Quarter which was mentioned in the last chapter. At that stage they may consider that they have had enough for one day.

Sharon Chapel

Another tour, a bit longer, can start at Warren's House again. This time visitors should keep Warren's on their left and travel along Highway 2. About a kilometre further along, they will come to Sharon Chapel which is in the parish of St. Thomas and was built by the Moravians in 1765. It attracts considerable attention with its tower and windows that are characteristic of the 18th Century.

Welchman Hall Gully

Welchman Hall Gully

A few kilometres away on Highway 2 is Welchman Hall Gully. This is a botanical ravine, luxuriant with plants and trees. It is a fascinating piece of indigenous woodland planted by an owner of the property many years ago. It is now owned by the Barbados National Trust who have taken great care to preserve its original character. At the northern approach to the Gully is a gazebo which looks out to the Atlantic Ocean.

Harrison's Cave

Near to Welchman Hall Gully is Harrison's Cave. The visitors are still in the parish of St. Thomas and here they will be tempted to linger for a while.

When they arrive at the entrance to the cavern, they will see the Visitors' Centre which is designed to fit in with the natural shape of the limestone bedrock. Visitors are provided with such facilities as an area for relaxation and for refreshments, a handicraft shop and an exhibit of Amerindian artifacts that have been excavated from various sites in the island.

Visitors are prepared for what lies before them by a five-minute colour slide show introducing them to the cavern. Then they board a special tram that takes them through subterranean stream passages. They will see a natural phenomenon that lies near the geographical centre of the island and will enjoy an unforgettable experience.

On board the tram visitors are accompanied by a driver and guide and set out on an underground drive lasting forty-five minutes. During that drive they will see bubbling streams, thundering waterfalls, tumbling cascades, deep pools and all the other features that

Stalactites and stalagmites in Harrisons Cave

make up the environment of the cavern. And all along the route bubbles the stream that originally formed the cavern.

When the lowest point in the cavern is reached, the visitors get out of the tram and walk alongside a waterfall that plunges into a blue pool twelve metres below. The cavern is almost one and a half kilometres long and they will see stalactites in countless numbers as well as stalagmites. The latter form the floor beneath the waters which, because of their special qualities, are constantly and actively forming them.

To enhance the spectacle of sight and sound, there are indirect lights that play around the waters which glisten and cascade on all sides. It may well be said that Harrison's Cave is a phenomenon of nature that is unique in the tropical world.

Turner's Hall Wood

After emerging from Harrison's Cave, we are back on Highway 2. On their left the visitors, who are now in the parish of St. Andrew, will see Mount Hillaby, the highest point in Barbados, rising to a height of 340 metres. On their right is Sturges, a high point which is conspicuous with its antenna serving CBC-TV and radio stations. Further ahead lies Turner's Hall Wood, which is almost inaccessible, but a visit to this area will amply reward the effort of more venturesome spirits.

When the English first settled here in 1627, most of the island was covered with primeval forest. Most of this has disappeared except in Turner's Hall Wood and some of the more remote gullies. In Turner's Hall Wood, intrepid visitors will see tall trees with vines stringing their canopies overhead. They will note such trees as locust, mastic, sand box, jack-in-the box, red cedar, spanish oak and cabbage palm.

Until some years ago the locust, mastic and red cedar trees were exploited for firewood, but fortunately this is now a thing of the past. The locust still grows in the Wood with its tall, straight trunks reaching a height of some thirty metres. It bears a thick pod and contains a vile-smelling pulp. Strangely enough, if the visitor eats the pulp, he will find it harmless and quite sweet and pleasant.

Another rare tree is the jack-in-the-box. It bears a small fruit with a hollow bladder. A seed stands erect from the base, about two centimetres long, and can be seen from a hole in the top of the fruit. It is from this that the tree derives its name. It has large heart-shaped leaves and its tall straight trunk gives it a magnificent appearance. This tree grows only in Turner's Hall Wood and can be found nowhere else in Barbados.

The cabbage palms, which have been compared with Grecian columns, can be seen in Turner's Hall Wood as well as in other inland woods. They are indigenous plants of great beauty and grow to immense heights. Graham Gooding has measured one of these trees in Turner's Hall Wood and established its height as forty metres.

The macaw palm is seen in several parts of Turner's Hall Wood and seems to thrive in very heavy shade. Visitors have to be careful not to step on fallen trunks or leaves since the tree is covered with long sharp spines. This tree, we are informed by Gooding, is endemic, that is to say its particular species, like the columnar cactus and maypole, is found nowhere else in the world.

The silk cotton tree grows with whorls of horizontal branches and reaches great heights in the woodland. It is described as a common native tree.

Mahogany trees also grow in Turner's Hall Wood but these need not be given any special notice since they are not native to the island and were therefore not part of the original woodland. But the tall, slender trees, known as wild clammy cherries, are part of the original Barbadian forest as distinct from the common clammy cherry which was imported from the Far East.

If the visitors have succeeded in reaching and penetrating Turner's Hall Wood, they should then return to Highway 2. Soon they will arrive at Haggatts. This was at first merely an Agricultural Station and a Stud Unit Station but is now the headquarters of the Soil Conservation and Rural Development Scheme in the Scotland District.

Started in 1957, it now employs 250 people to carry out its programme of soil conservation. It aims at producing fruit trees and encouraging the development of forestry. Its principal objective is to prevent soil slippage and soil erosion in the Scotland District which comprises St. Andrew and parts of the parishes of St. John and St. Joseph. This slippage or erosion is caused by a foundation of clay under the soil, which cannot be penetrated by water. The result is that the layer between the soil and the clay causes the soil to slip or be completely eroded.

To cope with this serious problem three methods are employed. First, grass is planted on the hillsides to bind the soil but a careful watch must be maintained to prevent sheep from pulling up the grass. Secondly, gabions, consisting of wire baskets filled with stones of various sizes, are built and placed wherever water is likely to flow. When the rains come, the water flows through the stones in the gabions and this slows down the onrush that takes the soil away with it. In addition, citrus fruit trees are widely distributed free of charge to help in the task of saving the soil in the area from slippage or erosion.

A visit to Haggatts is very worthwhile. It will show the visitor the activities in which it is engaged to save a district that represents as much as one-seventh of the island's entire surface.

Chalky Mount

Back on Highway 2, the visitors turn off on the right to the road leading to Coggins Hill which takes them right up to Chalky Mount. The public road takes them right into the Pottery Village. Here they can have various things made for them such as clay coal pots, miniature water jugs and flower pots.

The visitors have not yet reached the summit of the Mount which rises to 167 metres above sea level. A path leads them to the final steep rise which takes

A view of the Scotland District

them to the principal summit of Chalky Mount. The first part is easy going but to reach the main summit they have to cover a bit of terrain which is rendered difficult by the loose sandstone rocks. The more daring visitors who succeed in making it to the top will be rewarded by a magnificent view of the Scotland District.

This is generally regarded as a unique area in Barbados. It is a small mountain range of an interesting geological formation. It rises in bold relief, as Hutt has accurately described it, with a fine pinnacle ridge pointing to the Atlantic Ocean, with various subsidiary summits and ridges, and with fine broken cliffs facing both the north and the south.

If the visitors have succeeded in reaching the highest point of Chalky Mount, they can bring this particular tour to an end with a sense of achievement.

Further Reading
Report to Council of Barbados National Trust by Maurice Hutt (1975).
CBC-TV Lectures by Graham Gooding (unpublished).
Barbodos Diocesan History by J.E. Reece and C.G. Clark Hunt (1925).

Chapter Thirteen

FROM BRIDGETOWN TO ANDROMEDA

The tour suggested for today extends from Bridgetown to Andromeda Gardens on the east coast of the island. It takes visitors along a number of highways and byways and, since it will be a rather long journey, I suggest that before setting out, they should order lunch at one of such places as Atlantis Hotel, Bonita Bar, Edgewater Inn or Round House in Bathsheba or at Kingsley Club in Cattle Wash.

Visitors should set out from Bridgetown by Highway 4. After passing Rouen, they should turn away from the Highway into the pleasant, shady byway that leads through Salters. At the cross roads at the end of Salters, they should turn right and proceed up Rectory Hill until they reach St. George's Church at the end of this gentle incline.

St. George's Church

This may not be the loveliest church in the island but it contains a number of interesting treasures. There is a painting on copper of *The Descent from the Cross* in the north porch of the church. Its origin is not known but it is clearly of great age and its workmanship

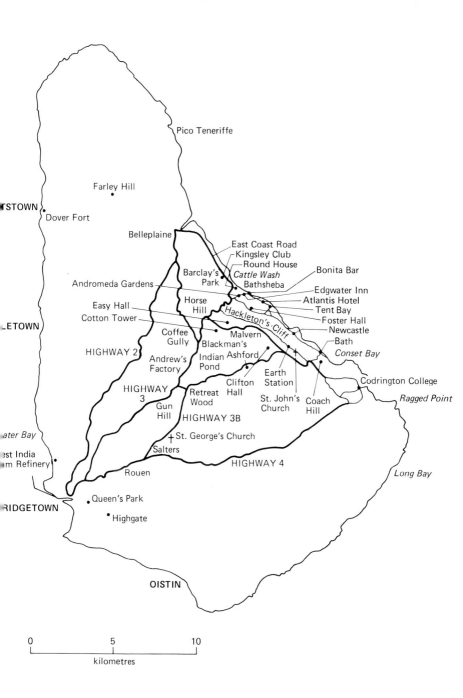

Map 10 From Bridgetown to Andromeda Gardens

117

bears the stamp of a Master.

Among the rich communion plate, there are large pieces of 17th century silver. There are, in addition, an immense flagon, two large patens, indentical in size, shape and workmanship and a pair of chalices, also identical in every respect. These articles bear the London hallmarks of 1679, 1691, and 1695 respectively.

Perhaps the most intriguing part of the church is the altar piece representing the resurrection, painted by the celebrated American artist, Benjamin West. There is a legend that, when the painting arrived in Barbados, a dispute arose between the Rector of the church and the donor, Mr. Frere, owner of Lower Estate. As a result of that dispute, the painting was stored in an outhouse at Lower Estate. While it was still in the outhouse, a carpenter broke in to steal something and pushed out the eye of the centurion because, he thought, the latter was watching him too vigilantly.

Unfortunately, by the time the picture was sent back to the artist to be restored, West was dead and *The Resurrection* was never properly repaired. Since 1923, however, a chancel has been added to the Church with four handsome stained-glass windows and a reredos frame in which West's masterpiece, with the centurion's damaged eye, has been suitably installed. This was mainly due to the generosity of a member of the congregation, The Honourable G.L. (later Sir Laurie) Pile.

Gunhill Signal Station

After leaving St. George's Church, the visitors travel up Gun Hill until they arrive at Gun Hill Signal Station. Standing out prominently from the hill is the lion carved from the island's natural limestone in 1868 by Henry Wilkinson. He was at the time Adjutant-General of the Imperial Forces stationed in Barbados.

The Gun Hill Station was then a signal post that was in constant communication with similar stations at Highgate in St. Michael, Montcrieffe on the border between St. John and St. Phillip, and Cotton Tower in St. Joseph. But it was also a convalescent station for the Imperial troops. Now, as then, the air is very salubrious and the station provides a view over a rich and fertile valley. The view extends east, west and south from Long Bay in St. Philip, to parts of Christ Church, St. Michael and St. George and on to Freshwater Bay where the Rum Refinery at Black Rock now stands.

There are two inscriptions on the Gun Hill monument. The first is in Latin which is translated as follows: 'It (i.e. the British Lion) shall rule from the rivers to the sea, and from the sea to the ends of the

The Lion Monument at Gun Hill

earth'; the name of the sculptor, his rank and date follow. The other inscription on the wall a little to the right of the Lion records the names of four military labourers who assisted Wilkinson in the work.

The Gun Hill Signal Station was recently leased to the Barbados National Trust and this is a guarantee that it will no longer be neglected as it had been during the past hundred years.

Cotton Tower

Travelling northward from Gun Hill, visitors pass Retreat Wood on their right, branch off to the left to get onto Highway 3B and then after a mile or less turn right onto Highway 3. This Highway leads them past Andrew's Factory and Coffee Gully on the left and Indian Ground and Blackman's on the right. When they get near the top of Horse Hill, they turn to the right into a byway that takes them to Cotton Tower.

Cotton Tower is a three-storey building about four metres square. Its floors, once of wood, are now of concrete. On the ground floor a plaque records when the first stone of the tower was laid and by whom, but it is almost completely illegible. Fortunately the attendant, Arthur Clarke, provides a leaflet with information collated by Edward Stoute, a member of the Council of the Barbados National Trust.

The data thus supplied informs visitors that the first stone of the Tower was laid during the administration of Lord Combermere, Governor of Barbados, and that the ceremony was performed in 1819 by his only daughter, the Honourable Caroline Frances Cotton after whom the Tower was named.

Cotton Tower is 332 metres above sea level and provides a clear view of the Scotland District and the East Coast Road which connects Cattle Wash to

Belleplaine. In the top storey there are two apertures, one pointing to Gun Hill and the other to Grenade Hall.

All messages originated from the General's residence in Queen's Park and were relayed by the hoisting of flags to St. Anne's Fort, then to Gun Hill and via Moncrieffe to Cotton Tower. The latter then signalled the messages to Grenade Hall, now a ruin on the site where Farley Hill now stands, and thence to Dover Fort in Speightstown. Dover Fort then sent the messages to the forts and batteries along the west coast alerting them for a possible attack from hostile ships.

Hackleton's Cliff

From Cotton Tower, the visitors move along byways first to Easy Hall and then to Malvern. By the side of this old plantation house is a long, narrow track leading to Hackleton's Cliff.

The experts tell us that, when the island first emerged from the sea, its entire surface was covered by a coral cap. Then there were upheavals in the sea, causing immense tidal waves which beat upon the eastern side of the island. So mighty was the force of the sea and so terrible the damage done by the waves that the coral cap was destroyed in the whole area now known as the Scotland District. This is said to have happened several million years ago.

Hackleton's Cliff is thus a geological phenomenon. It rises to some 305 metres above sea level and overlooks the whole area which was once submerged by raging torrents but from which the waters withdrew many, many years ago. It provides a view from Pico Teneriffe in the north to Ragged Point in the east. From the Cliff can be seen what has been described as 'the most perfect prospect on the island.'

It is small wonder that a Canadian visitor, who was once being shown around by Edward Stoute, was moved to say: 'In Canada we have the Niagara Falls, but in Barbados you have Hackleton's Cliff.'

St. John's Church

After leaving Hackleton's Cliff, the visitors return to the byway which leads them from Malvern to Clifton Hall, an impressive old plantation house conspicuous with its whitewood trees. A short distance away is St. John's Church with its frangipani trees spreading their pleasant scent all over the churchyard.

With its double staircase of light coloured cedar providing access to the organ gallery above, the tombs of planters who once ruled the land and the high-backed pews that are among the island's best antiques, it is one of the most handsome churches the visitor will find in Barbados. Its beauty is enhanced by the view it offers of the countryside beneath it and the giant Atlantic rollers that are ever breaking over the reefs beyond.

More particularly, the St. John's churchyard provides a clear view of two of the most famous health resorts in the island. First, there is Bathsheba and beyond it is Cattle Wash. Beyond Cattle Wash is Barclay's Park, a pleasant woodland where visitors, if they have not made other plans, can have a picnic lunch in true Barbadian style. But they must pay heed to the warnings that the sea in this area is very dangerous for bathing.

Bathsheba, Cattlewash and the East Coast Road offer splendid landscapes. With its salubrious climate and the fresh breezes blowing from the Atlantic Ocean, it is an area long known as one of the best

St. John's Church

health resort areas in Barbados and elsewhere in the
Caribbean. If visitors wish to linger in the district
they could visit the quaint fishing village at Trent
Bay. They will be enchanted with the view of the
coastline and numerous rocks detached from the

shore with the sea breaking over them sending cascades of foam high into the air.

One of the most famous graves in the churchyard of St. John's is that of Ferdinando Paleologus, a descendant of the Imperial line of the last Christian Emperors of Greece. He fought on the side of the Royalists in the English Civil War and, after the battle of Naseby in 1645, he came out as a refugee to Barbados where his mother's father owned property. For twenty years, according to the vestry minutes that are extant, he served on the Vestry of St. John. He lived in Ashford, St. John, now a bird park, until his death in 1678. This park, with its variety of bird life, is well worth a visit.

The inscription on his tombstone in St. John's churchyard is similar to that on his father's tomb in the Church of Landulph in Cornwall. It is not without significance that the view of the coast that can be seen from this churchyard was compared with that of Cornwall by Sir Frederick Treves in his classic, 'The Cradle of the Deep'.

Codrington College

After the visitors depart from St. John's Church, they should turn to the left and after a few minutes they will come to Coach Hill. When they descend this hill, they will come to Sergeant Street which will take them, within five minutes, to Codrington College.

The driveway into the College is lined with tall cabbage palm trees. When they reach the lake, near which an old silk cotton tree stands as a sentinel, they will see on their left the Principal's Lodge where the founder of the College, Christopher Codrington was born in 1668 and where, after a short, brilliant and troubled period, he died in 1710.

The College was established, in accordance with the will of the founder, to provide for the material and spiritual needs of the Negroes and Indians in the Caribbean area. The theological seminary he envisaged was to train missionaries not only in divinity but in 'physic and chirurgery'. His aim was that, by looking after men's bodies, the missionaries would endear themselves to the people and thus have a better opportunity to do good to their souls.

Today, the College, first started as the Codrington Grammar School in 1745, continues its work as intended by the founder. It has played a great part in the cause of education and the Church and its influence has spread from the most northerly part of the Caribbean down to Guyana. In 1875 it was affiliated to the University of Durham, England, and since 1965 it has been an integral part of the University of the West Indies.

The architecture of the College, with its un-

Codrington College

completed Oxford quadrangle, will interest the visitors. So will the rare treasures in the College Chapel. The glass mosaic of the Good Shepherd over the altar, the brass chandelier with the name of the donor inscribed on it, the lectern which was subscribed for by the Bishops of the West Indian province, the massive mahogany sanctuary rails and gates, the altar with its pedestals of ebony, cordia and lignum vitae, the brass tablet to the memory of the founder, the names of former Principals and tutors inscribed on other tablets in the stalls: these are only some of the things that enhance the beauty of the College Chapel and give it some claim to be a unique shrine in the West Indies.

Bath, Satellite And Poor Whites

If the visitors return along Sergeant Street, instead of going back up Coach Hill, they should turn to the right and go down Bath Hill. They will soon come to the ruins of Bath Factory and they should then turn off to the right and go downhill to the Bath Facility. Here they will find a large car park, a woodland mostly of casuarina trees and one of the safest bathing spots in the whole of the east coast. It is an ideal place for a bathe in the sea and a picnic lunch under the shade of the woods.

After this diversion, the tour can be continued westward. Within sight of the ruins of Bath Factory is the Barbados Earth Station where Cable And Wireless (Barbados) Limited provides us with satellite communication. The vast dish at the Station sends signals to the satellite which amplifies them and transmits them back to earth to several receiving countries in North America and Europe. With sophisticated ground equipment, these countries can

Barbados Earth Station

reproduce the signals and make them available to the general public in the form of T.V. programmes, telephone messages and computer calculations.

As a result of all this, Barbados now has the most modern communications within the Caribbean and South American area.

Why, it may be asked, has the island been chosen as the site of such a station? The answer may well lie in such factors as its geographical position, its educated populace and its long tradition of stable government.

Further along the way we come to Newcastle. Here and in other parts of the Scotland District, visitors will see small communities of poor whites or 'redlegs'. They are so called because they used to wear kilts while working in the canefields, their legs becoming sunburnt as a result of this practice.

Supposedly of Scottish origin, they and their ancestors have been in Barbados for more than 300 years. They appear to be trapped in their poverty and seem to have been relegated to the lowest rung of the social ladder in Barbados. They are a strange breed of people and are referred to by such pejorative names as Scotland Johnnies, Backra Johnnies and White Niggers.

Soon we are in Foster Hall with its approach and its exit marked by avenues of coconut trees. And, after one or two sweeping bends, we arrive at Andromeda which is the final stop in our present tour.

Further Reading
Barbados Diocesan History by J.E. Reece and C.G. Clark-Hunt (1925).
Note on Cotton Tower by Edward Stoute (unpublished).
Annals of Codrington College by T.H. Bindley (1911).

Chapter Fourteen

ANDROMEDA GARDENS

Andromeda Gardens deserve a separate chapter to do justice to their beauty. They are, indeed, a perennial source of delight. For at all times of the year there are many things to be seen in bloom and bright leaf.

Andromeda was started by Iris Bannochie in 1954 and she is still its presiding genius, enthusiastically assisted by her husband, John.

Many Years Ago

Like the maiden in the Greek legend, from whom their name is derived, Andromeda Gardens are tied to a rock or rather a series of giant boulders. As a result of the upheavals mentioned in the previous chapter, these boulders came tumbling down and were deposited in the valley many, many years ago. They are now at rest, firmly embedded in a rich clay, sometimes as much as nine metres in depth.

All that remains of the great cataracts, which once brought the boulders down from Hackleton's Cliff, is the small stream or rivulet which meanders through the Gardens and then goes cascading down to the quaint fishing village at Tent Bay in Bathsheba and

Andromeda Gardens

thence to the vast expanse of the Atlantic Ocean.

Andromeda was also associated with the ancient civilisation of the Amerindians who once lived in Barbados. For when the foundation of the house and the holes for the trees at Andromeda were being prepared, various artifacts of these peoples were found, namely: axes, hoes, chisels, spears, tools and pottery.

Prominent among the trees in Andromeda is the magificent banyan, known, more popularly, as the bearded fig tree. There are other trees that once formed part of the primeval forest that once covered the surface of the island. These include fustic, whitewood, pop-a-gun and maypole trees.

Interesting Features

The house at Andromeda was completed a year after

Hibiscus

its building was started. By that time the work of planting and landscaping was well on its way. There were two interesting features. One field, which was comparatively flat and irrigated by the spring and rivulet, had by then been transformed into a flourishing vegetable garden. The second feature was a hydroponic system which was designed to grow tomatoes at all seasons of the year. Today the vegetable garden is a nursery for ornamental plants and the seven long hydroponic bays serve as a mist-propagator for the nursery.

At the beginning, a lawn was established to set off the house at Andromeda. The soil, which was excavated to make the lawn, left a hole in the ground and this hole is now the big lily pond which is crossed by a causeway. This ingenious arrangement permits the uninhibited growth of both day-blooming and night-blooming water lilies. For, if they were planted in the same place, the day-blooming water lilies would crowd out those that bloom by night.

The plants were always the important personalities in this garden of Andromeda, and in the landscaping the protection and love given to the plants provided them with every chance to adapt to their new home.

There were other tasks that called for urgent attention. It was essential to protect the stream bed from the floods that had caused disastrous erosion over the years so rough walls were built to hold up the banks of the stream. The business of conservation and proper drainage is a never-ending one in order to protect the garden.

Bridges And Paths

The work of extending and improving Andromeda was to prove a source of immeasurable pleasure to Iris and John Bannochie. Bridges were built, crossing over to several points where the soil was rich and the area for planting more extensive. Paths were made, leading up, down and across, designed in such a way as to avoid monotony and suit the varying moods of Andromeda.

It is in the construction of quaint bridges and meandering paths that the Bannochies have shown a great deal of ingenuity and imagination.

Some of these paths are of brick and local sandstone. Others are grassed, wherever the terrain allows, while others again are of concrete slabs which are skilfully imprinted with the veined leaves of the plants in the gardens.

Varying Climates And Soils

Strange as it may seem, there are many climates and a variety of soil conditions in the gardens of

Andromeda. For this reason it was important to group the various plants according to the cultural conditions they required. It is true that there is always a breeze, blowing from the Atlantic, to cool and refresh the plants; yet the tropical sun, when it beats down fiercely upon them, makes it necessary to have shady retreats at various points to protect plants and gardeners alike.

Begonias And Hibiscus

Begonias were planted, with the white begonia as a special favourite for hedges in semi-shady areas. Bougainvillaeas were also cultivated and soon they were scrambling up trees and cascading down hillsides. Now adding to the colourful display are red ginger lilies, growing along the banks of the stream, together with the brilliant torch ginger lilies and the crimson pineapple ginger lilies.

Frangipani

In 1956 a swimming pool was built and a terraced garden was created from the excavated soil. The first flowers that appeared here were the hibiscus which is regarded as one of the symbols of the tropics. For they last only one day and yet are in bloom every day of the year.

Soon the hibiscus plants, with more than a hundred varieties, were too much for the terraced garden. Accordingly, the area around the swimming pool was levelled and covered with grass and this, along with the gently sloping and well-drained land above it, proved to be an ideal site to spread out the rapidly proliferating hibiscus plants.

Continuing Expansion

The work of expansion continued at Andromeda. Another lily pond was built in an area almost completely surrounded by rocks. The bearded fig tree is close to this pond and at one time marked the end of Andromeda Gardens on the southern side. In 1966, however, paths were constructed among the huge boulders leading to the top of Andromeda. With a rare gift for improvisation, the Bannochies diverted a natural spring to flow cascading along a prepared path and thence into the pond. The result is that the large coral-stone rocks, once formidable in their sterility, now appear to be congenial hosts to cactus and other similar succulents in little sheltered pockets.

A Complete Contrast

Next to the garden of the huge boulders, another garden was established on a gently sloping area of deep rich soil. To accomplish this a rubbish dump had to be removed and some dense trees pruned and thinned to allow the sunlight to come through.

To establish this new garden, which is now a complete contrast to the garden of the giant rocks, another path was built. It starts near the swimming pool, runs along the river course, and winds through the Heliconia Garden. It passes the old breadfruit, pop-a-gun and fustic trees on the right and the open area on the left. It then joins the bearded fig path at two points which both lead down through the Hibiscus Garden. Two long ponds, with a waterfall between them, nestle under a natural rocky escarpment.

While these things were being developed up the hill, the work of creation was going steadily ahead in the central and bottom areas of Andromeda. Bamboos and casuarinas were planted to take the place of the original coconut palm windbreaks. The palm garden was established and increases every year with new species added from all over the tropics. Already it dominates this part of Andromeda and a list is posted at the entrance with the names of the various species.

The Aristocrats

A visit to South East Asia inspired Iris Bannochie to establish an orchid garden at Andromeda. A favourable place for these aristocrats of the plant kingdom was found in a sheltered mini-valley which lay in the path of a moist, warm current of air moving towards a number of large limestone boulders. This spot was incorporated with the terraced garden below the swimming pool. Today this area is entirely devoted to the cultivation of orchids which are naturally landscaped and which provide a colourful display throughout the year.

Ixora, Flame of the Woods

The growth of the orchid garden has been such that it is now merged with the orchid houses across the stream. Orchids grow on the trunks of avocado, breadfruit and Barbados cherry trees. They grow in pots or baskets and on rafts that are hung under trees that serve as their hosts.

Spreading Fame

Thus the gardens of Andromeda have flourished and their fame spread to various parts of the world. The horticultural wealth of the gardens could not have grown without the plants that have been introduced from many countries in the Caribbean and beyond.

The flow of plant material, however, has been a two way traffic. Plants from Andromeda have been sent abroad and are now growing in the Royal Botanic Garden at Kew, in the greenhouses of the Brighton Parks and Garden Department, in the Long-wood Gardens in Philadelphia, in the Hidden Lake Gardens in Michigan as well as nearly all the territories of the Caribbean and many other parts of the world.

Haven Of Peace

Thus the growth and transformation of Andromeda has taken place over the years. Andromeda now occupies an area of four and a half hectares (ten acres). Once overgrown with bush and weeds, it is now beautified with the lush growth of ginger lilies and ixoras, with oleanders and begonias, with crotons and aralias and with bougainvillaeas, some of them from Kenya, scrambling up trees and cascading down miniature hillsides.

There are such things as lovely purple leaves, silvering in the sunlight, forget-me-nots, watercress and ferns in places through which the sunlight filters, grasses for different situations such as sun and shade, shallow soils and well trodden paths, which mingle and mix their yellows and greens in fascinating patterns.

The terraces, the hills and the mini-valleys, the colour and the variety and the stark contrasts make Andromeda Gardens the highlight of any tour in Barbados. It is small wonder that visitors from many parts of the world have paid glowing tributes to the remarkable phenomenon that is Andromeda.

'There are times,' wrote a visitor,' 'when we all wish that fairy tales come true. Times when we long to come upon the door of enchantment, the escape route from the world of noise, strain and tedium, leading to a haven of peace and serenity. The other day I found one. It was the Garden of Andromeda.'

Further Reading
A Garden Called Andromeda by Iris Bannochie (unpublished).

Chapter Fifteen

WHEN NIGHT FALLS

Many visitors, after a long day in the sun, will be looking for entertainment when the shadows of evening begin to darken the scene. Barbados has much to offer those who are in search of the pleasures that night brings in this tropical paradise.

The Hotels

Night life in the island is centred mainly around the hotels which present after-dinner shows with local

The Hilton Hotel

bands and floor performances. The chief attractions here are the fire-eaters, the belly dancers and those extraordinary artists who perform their wondrous feats under a flaming rod that is sometimes only six inches from the ground. They move forward towards the bar, first bending their knees and then leaning backwards. Their bodies almost touch the ground and they dance slowly towards the rod and then beneath the searing flames.

The limbo reflects part of the native culture of Barbados. It is a blend of an African dance form, which has survived since the sombre régime of slavery, and the Caribbean calypso of later and happier times. So captivated are visitors by the limbo that they try to do it themselves and take innumerable pictures of the performance.

Among the hotels that provide such entertainment are Sandy Lane, Colony Club, Sunset Crest and Miramar on the west coast, South Winds, Rockley Resort and Hilton on the south and Silver Sands and Sam Lord's on the east.

Restaurants

There are many restaurants to cater for the varying needs of visitors. Among those that are well worth a visit are Brown Sugar, Captain's Carbery, Chateau Creole, Flamboyant International Flower Drum, Foolish Fish, Green House and Green Sleeves. Among many others also worthy of mention are Luigi's, Pisces, Plantation Restaurant, Sand Dollar, Water Garden Restaurant, the Witch Doctor and the Fort Charles Restaurant at the Hilton. At these restaurants a large variety of fare is offered. This fare includes authentic West Indian cuisine, the finest imported as well as local fruits and vegetables, exotic dishes prepared in the Creole manner, the hot spicy cuisine of South-West China and à la carte menus with local, West Indian and continental specialties to satisfy the most discriminating tastes.

The Pepper Pot

If hotel guests desire something different, they will venture out to the larger night-clubs in the island. One of the best known of these is the Caribbean Pepperpot where visitors, especially those from temperate climates, love to dance in the open air, under the stars.

Chief among those who provide the music here are the Merrymen, Ivory, Spice, Escorts and Night Life. In addition to this, there is a floor show which is accompanied by disco music and the Elks Steel Band.

The Merrymen

The Merrymen have become one of the institutions of Barbados. They have researched the legends and folklore of the island and brought them to life with their music. Their lyrics have established them as the pioneers in this field and, wherever they go in their musical journey from Barbados to Europe and North America, they are regarded as among the best ambassadors of the island.

Lord Radio

Among those who make appearances at the Pepperpot and other places is Lord Radio, one of the leading personalities in the field of calypso and folk song.

In 1981 he celebrated his twenty-fifth anniversary

as an entertainer in the hotel circuit. His popularity is due to his gift for improvising song and his genius for administering 'picong', the gentle Trinidad art of leg-pulling.

Calypso And Folk Song

Most visitors, who have probably had more than their fill of North American jazz, are on the look out for calypso music. Such entertainment is provided by the Reunion and other calypso bands already mentioned which provide the island music that 'sends' visitors and induces them to join spontaneously in the 'jump-up'.

A number of hotels, particularly Sunset Crest, Southern Palms and Silver Sands, provide such music. In addition, there are the folk singers. Among the better known are Cavite Chorale and Sing Out Barbados at the Hilton. These are large mixed choirs which specialise in Caribbean folk songs.

The Island Inn

One of the most frequented night spots is the Island

Local entertainment — limbo dancing

Inn. It has a longer history than any other similar place in the field of entertainment and provides the best example of floor shows that are native to the Caribbean.

The Island Inn is more accurately referred to as a night spot than as a night-club since its entertainment is offered mostly on Monday night. If visitors are looking for something with a genuine local flavour, the Island Inn is the answer to their quest. Indeed, many of them have already discovered that it is here they can enjoy an outstanding entertainment programme. To them Island Inn and Monday night have become synonymous terms. Among those who have made the discovery, it has become almost a slogan: 'On Monday night it's Island Inn.'

Local Haunts

There are night-clubs like the Banana Boat which promote special nights designed to feature well-established artists. Those who wish to explore local haunts that do not cater specifically to visitors, might care to venture into the International Disco to hear Wendy Alleyne and The Dynamics or to listen to the Blue Ribbon Combo in their disco, Studio Ten.

Discos

Visitors will also want to visit the discos which are very popular. These are comparable in atmosphere, style and character of entertainment with popular discos in any major city. The latest popular music is available and this, combined with reggae and calypso, provide a nicely mixed programme of entertainment. In addition, tropical drinks are served that are guaranteed to produce a high level of excitement.

Dancing at a night spot

The Stables, which is connected with the Plantation Restaurant, is a disco-cum-pub where conversation is possible because the music and dance areas are separated by sound-proof glass. In the outdoor section is the 'mechanical bull', the only one in the West Indies, which provides much hilarity for both riders and onlookers.

Other discos are the Hippo, the Rendezvous Room in the Rockley Beach Resort Hotel, the Unicorn I in the Southern Palms and the Flambeau Bar at the Hilton.

For those who want a contrast there are a few piano bars, such as the Music Man Inn and Rockley Resort, and small groups such as Velvet which play soft and moody contemporary music.

English Pubs

Visitors who would like to savour the atmosphere of

an English Pub, may choose many places such as the Coach House, the Mill Pub and Restaurant, and the Cricketers at Coconut Creek Hotel on the west coast. The Ship and the Windsor Arms lie on the south coast.

Here they will experience the genuine flavour of an English pub. They can sit around the counter and drink their 'pint' in the manner of all the other patrons. And in no time they will be warmed by the hospitality of the place.

The Steel Bands

Where, the visitors frequently ask, are the steel bands, the native troubadours of the island? It is the question asked by the thousands and tens of thousands that come to Barbados. For they have heard of the unique instruments used by these bands and the high quality of the music produced by these instruments.

Whilst the steel band was developed in Trinidad, it

Local entertainment — a group

is also popular in Barbados. Oil drums were transformed into musical instruments by a simple process. Their bottoms were marked out into various sections. Each of these sections was so fashioned as to produce an individual tone and then they were blended together into a remarkable harmony and melody.

The quality and variety of the music produced by the steel bands never fails to amaze and captivate the visitors to our shores. For their skill and artistry take them through a remarkable repertoire; from the classical movements of Tchaikowski and Mozart to the throbbing rhythms of the Caribbean calypso.

The Barbados All Stars Steel Orchestra

The steel bands may be found in the various hotels. But those who are looking for the best should attend the performances of the Barbados All Stars Steel Orchestra at Paradise Beach on Fridays, Sunset Crest on Sundays and Southern Palms at lunch-time every Sunday.

There is no more talented band playing this type of music than the Barbados Steel Orchestra. By its skill, it has elevated the steel band music to the status of an art form. It has accompanied officials of the Board of Tourism on tours during the past seven years and has won an international reputation in Canada, the United States and Europe.

On one unforgettable occasion, the Orchestra performed in Vienna and played three movements from one of Mozart's famous compositions. It was the first time such a performance had been given by a steel band and the Barbados Orchestra was given a warm and sustained standing ovation that brought tears of joy to their eyes.

The Tuk Band

The tuk band represents one of the healthy traditions of Barbados. It is a part of the island's cultural, historic and ethnic heritage. Like the limbo, it is a happy survival of the gloomy days of slavery. It dates from a time when the slaves were forbidden to use drums, horns and other loud instruments. The Koromantin drum was specifically prohibited because its 'terrors' were likely to throw the island's white inhabitants into a state of panic.

From all this the tuk band emerged when the slaves were forced to adapt their ethnic music to British military instruments. The band consists, in the main, of three musicians: the penny – whistle player sets the tune and tempo, the kettle – drummer changes the movements and style of the music and the bass drummer produces the hearty bass sound. Others added to the band, especially on festive occasions, are the Donkey Man, the Stilt Man and Mother Sally. The music and the costumes on these occasions reflect colourful aspects of the authentic folk culture of Barbados.

The leading tuk band was taken by the Board of Tourism on its tour of Europe in 1980. They visited Vienna, Zurich and Amsterdam as well as many cities in West Germany. Wherever they went, they were given a great reception.

Bajan Night

Both Sam Lord's Castle and the Hilton put on a Bajan Night event. A typical Bajan Village and the 'rum-shop' are re-created with authentic props — the board and shingle cottage; the lounging inhabitants and, perhaps above all, the Mauby Woman, with a small

A Rum Shop

cask on her head, ever ready and willing to turn on the tap to slake the thirst of visitors with the genuine article.

Cultural And Folkloric Shows

Visitors who want to enjoy an evening with a difference are advised to visit the Barbados Museum on Thursday and Sunday evenings when they can attend the performance of *1627 And All That Sort of Thing.* The performance is preceded by a tour of the Museum and a buffet dinner.

On such an occasion, the visitors feel the Museum open air courtyard is an ideal place to be and there is a sense of excitement about what is to come. They watch the local folk dancers perform the history of Barbados through dance.

Barbados, Barbados

Another show has been designed by the genius of Andrew Nehaul. It is based on the life of Rachel Pringle, one of the most picaresque personalities in the island's history. It is a musical comedy and is presented every Tuesday evening from 6.30 to 10 p.m.. It has a remarkable setting in the old boiling house of Balls Plantation.

The Garden Theatre

The Garden Theatre is sited in the grounds of the Plantation Restaurant amid its majestic mahogany trees. It presents its Tropical Spectacular every Wednesday. There are two performances. The first is a dinner-buffet show, starting at 6 p.m., and the second a cocktail show, commencing at 9.30 p.m. The Merrymen give their own performance every Tuesday evening, starting at 8.30 p.m.

The scenario of Tropical Spectacular is the first presentation of its kind in Barbados on a professional stage equipped with theatrical lighting. The costumes are delightfully colourful and the entire musical score is arranged and performed by 'Spice', a young, talented and highly acclaimed group. The producer of the show is Emil Straker and his wife, Joyce, is the co-ordinator.

The show is based on the folklore and historical legend of Barbados. In the style of the Folie Bergère of Paris, the Sugar Mill Plantation Dancers depict, in mime and dance, the revelry of the Amerindians, the first settlers of Barbados. Then they take the audience to the boisterous days of the buccaneers who roamed the high seas of the Caribbean. The story they tell would be incomplete without appropriate reference to

Sam Lord, the notorious character, of whom mention has already been made in this narrative.

The era of buccaneers and shipwrecks and treasures is presented in a stage setting with ultra violet lights enhancing the eeriness of a moonlit night when spirits and wraiths can be expected to roam at will.

The scene is then switched to plantation life performed by The Barbados Dance Theatre in mime and dance, recalling old traditions of a bygone age. The climax is the celebration of Crop Over which is a happy and infectious scene with the Donkey Woman, the Stiltman and all the workers celebrating to the jump-up music of a tuk band.

The Castle Dinner

The castle dinner at Sam Lord's Castle will probably be a unique experience for those who have the opportunity to attend it. When Queen Elizabeth II came to Barbados in 1977, she was entertained at Sam Lord's Castle by the Prime Minister, Tom Adams.

To commemorate that event, Sam Lord's Castle has held a castle dinner every Wednesday evening for its guests. Usually, a Barbadian couple is invited to honour the occasion and to help entertain the guests.

Those whose imagination is in good working order, may well think that Sam Lord himself is present on that occasion. The large mahogany dining table, the dinner service, the chandelier overhead and the pictures and mirrors around certainly remind us of the days when Sam entertained his friends with lavish hospitality.

On the floor above the dining room is Sam's bedroom with his massive four-poster and large wardrobe. And, according to the evidence of two old ladies of many years ago, his ghost can still be seen in and around that room.

As the visitors look across the grounds to the ocean, they may well ask themselves the ever-recurring questions. Did Sam hang lanterns in those swaying coconut trees to lure ships on to the Cobblers Reef? And did he, from the plunder of those ships, acquire the ill-gotten gains to build his castle?

The *Jolly Rogers*

Visitors who have been captivated by the spirit of the castle dinner will be enthralled by the atmosphere of the 'pirate' ships, *Jolly Roger I* and *II*.

As soon as they board any of those vessels, they realise they are on a 'pirate' cruise and in a 'pirate' atmosphere and they let their hair down without any inducement. There is food and drink a plenty. Visitors enjoy the 'pirate' wedding when the Captain, with his authority to perform a wedding ceremony,

The Two Jolly Rogers

marries two volunteers who stay married for the duration of the cruise.

Visitors sail down the west coast with the trade wind blowing gently on their faces. If it is an afternoon cruise, they see the sun set on the horizon across the vast expanse of the ocean. If they sail at night, they have the light of the moon to add glamour to the occasion. The spirit of jollification is enhanced by the music of the Merrymen, Spice, Night Life with Carolyn Leacock and the V.S.O.P. Dixie Land Jazz Band.

Captain Patch

Captain Patch is not a sister ship of the *Jolly Roger I* and *II*. It provides visitors with a different kind of cruise which is quieter and more relaxed. In fact, it is claimed, without seeking to be invidious, that they sail 'for the cruise and not for the booze'.

The route of *Captain Patch* takes her into Carlisle Bay where she docks for lunch and enables her guests to indulge in snorkelling and other water sports. After lunch she sails smoothly along the west coast and, when she docks, those who are so inclined may enjoy a swim in the clear waters of the Caribbean.

The attractions *Captain Patch* offers would not be complete without the steel band which provides the music that is appropriate to the occasion.

Bel Air

Just a stone's throw from Harry's Nitery, which claims world-wide fame or notoriety because of its 'naughty' shows, there is the famous Bel Air Jazz Club on Bay Street. It is a late late night spot which comes to life at eleven p.m.

It caters to an interesting cross-section of people. There you will meet business executives, public servants and members of the learned professions. Indeed, you will meet all sorts from the highest to the less exalted gradations of Barbadian society.

The atmosphere is casual, unpretentious and relaxed. Visitors are given a hearty welcome and they join, without let or hindrance, in the cameraderie which is one of the special characteristics of Bel Air.

More Genteel

The eminent respectability of Bel Air cannot be questioned. Yet, if you want more genteel entertainment, you can attend the occasional live stage show by visiting artists or by the Barbados Dance Theatre during their season of dance.

In addition, the Barbados Symphonia does a concert from time to time; and the Green Room and other smaller drama groups provide good theatrical offerings.

Finale

When you have tasted all the delights that the night spots have to offer, you must at some time or other end up at Collins or Enid's in Baxters Road. For it is there that you will enjoy the full flavour of down to earth Barbadian night life. These are the haunts where all the beautiful people meet when they have had their surfeit of all the other pleasures of the night.

There is good local food at reasonable prices. Local people abound and visitors are cordially welcomed. You will enjoy the small rum shops, the spicy local food and the loud juke-box music. And if you join in the spirit of Baxters Road, you will linger until the early hours and dance around, swinging to the vibrations of the street that never sleeps.

Further Reading
Barbados. Things You Should Know compiled by the Barbados Board of Tourism.
Barbados Tourist News published by the Carib Publicity Company Ltd.
Caribjet Inflight magazine of Caribbean Airways.
Time Out published by Joint Marketing and Publishing Services Ltd.
Visitor published by The Nation newspaper.

Authors Note This section represents a cross section of entertainment provided on the island at the time of writing. For more detailed information the visitor should refer to the above publications and the daily newspapers (Advocate-News, The Nation).

INDEX

155

158

160